It is impossible NOT to encounter the R
small in number of pages, but huge in cor
spiritual disciplines, types of prayer, ai
fuel the life of a disciple.

LEE NAGEL, *Executive Director, National Conference for Catechetical Leadership*

This book is a powerful guide for us all, whether we're catechists, pastoral ministers, or anyone seeking God.

BILL HUEBSCH, *author of* ***Whole Community Catechesis in Plain English*** *and director of pastoralplanning.com*

Wonderfully practical and spiritually enriching. The section on prayer alone is worth the price of the book.

NEIL PARENT, *Past Executive Director of the National Conference for Catechetical Leadership; Past Project Director, Emerging Models of Pastoral Leadership, National Association for Lay Ministry*

This book presents spiritual insights and wisdom that will benefit everyone engaged in Christian ministry.

JOHN ROBERTO, *LifelongFaith Associates, editor,* ***Lifelong Faith Journal***

Janet has captured the essential element that sets apart a witness who transmits the faith through invitation into relationship with Jesus Christ from a mere teacher.

BRIAN A. LEMOI, *Executive Director, Department of Evangelization & Lifelong Faith Formation, Diocese of St. Petersburg*

This is an amazing book, amazing in its content, amazing in its format, and amazing in its clear and 100% reader-friendly style. It is a treasure chest for everyone engaged in catechesis in any way!

MELANNIE SVOBODA, SND, *author of* ***Everyday Epiphanies*** *and* ***When the Rain Speaks***

This is a delightful gift to the catechetical community and to all who are interested in spiritual formation.

DANIEL S. MULHALL, *Catechist, Author:* ***Let God Build the House, 8 Steps for Effective Pastoral Planning***

A catechist has been described as one who facilitates communication between people and the mystery of God and with one another (GDC 156). Janet does just that, and she gently and wisely leads us to do the same.

Suzanne Nelson, *Adult Faith Formation Coordinator, St. Raphael Parish, Rockville, MD*

Truly accessible, inspiring, and practical, this is a critical resource for catechists who know the heart of their vocation is who they are as disciples of Jesus.

Dr. Carole Eipers, *Vice President, Executive Director of Catechetics at William H. Sadlier, Inc. and author of* ***Catechist 101: Wade Don't Dive***

I hope Parish Catechetical Leaders would use this book as prayer for their meetings, as a catechist retreat, or an evening of prayer.

Mary Ann Ronan *retired Catechetical Leader and Past President of the Board of Directors for the National Conference of Catechetical Leaders*

Janet beautifully explores the tradition of Christian spirituality and the practices of prayer in clear and practical ways.

Daniel J. Pierson, *founder of eCatechist.com & faithAlivebooks.com*

This is a gem of a book, leading us to introspection about our spirituality, our holiness, and our journey to live up to what we became at baptism.

Dr. Lorraine S. DeLuca, *Director, Evangelization and Catechesis, Diocese of Beaumont*

Through the discussion questions and action steps in each chapter, Janet invites readers to go deeper in a way that is achievable for any adult.

Pam Coster, *Executive Director, Charis Ministries*

I have not seen a better history, explanation, guide, or assistant than this book offers. You'll want to read it more than once!

Anne Comeaux, *Past President of the National Conference for Catechetical Leadership and former director of the catechetical office in the Archdiocese of Galveston-Houston and the Diocese of Wheeling-Charleston*

A practical invitation to companionship in prayer and to grow in holiness, this book makes a perfect gift for catechists of all ages.

José M. Amaya, *Director of Faith Formation, Archdiocese for the Military Services, USA*

The ESSENTIAL CATECHIST'S BOOKSHELF

THE Spirituality OF THE CATECHIST

FEEDING YOUR SOUL,
GROWING *in* FAITH,
SHARING *with* OTHERS

Janet Schaeffler, OP

Dedication

To my mom and dad, who modeled for me
a trusting, compassionate spirituality

and to the Adrian Dominican Sisters,
who continue to nurture a prophetic
visionary spirituality centered
in community and care.

Twenty-Third Publications
1 Montauk Avenue, Suite 200, New London, CT 06320
(860) 437-3012 » (800) 321-0411 » www.23rdpublications.com

ISBN: 978-1-58595-949-5
Library of Congress Catalog Card Number: 2013957105
Printed in the U.S.A.

Contents

Introduction

Why a book on the spirituality of the catechist—all catechists, including those who minister with adults of all ages and stages of life, and those who minister with youth and children? We may feel that we need books on "what to teach," books with many and varied ideas of methods and activities, and books about how to facilitate a catechetical session. We do!

Yet something comes before these crucial components. Who we are speaks much louder than all that we say. We are called to be catechists, to echo and re-echo Jesus Christ and the good news that Jesus taught and lived.

We cannot give what we do not have. If someone asked us for five dollars, could we give it if we didn't have it? If someone asked us to listen, could we do that if we've never slowed down enough to be attentive to what others have to say?

We give what we have. As faith-filled Christians, we have been gifted with so much. As committed disciples, we are challenged to act. As dedicated catechists, we are called to journey with others. The depth and richness of our spirituality is the foundation for who we are, for all that we do. We live authentically and walk generously with others because of our spirituality.

We are called, especially because of our ministry as catechists, to grow and deepen our spirituality. "Like all the faithful, catechists are called to holiness. Because of their ministry and mission, however, the call to holiness has a particular urgency" (*National Directory for Catechesis,* 54.b.8). What a gift! What a challenge!

This book is designed to accompany each of us on our journey in spirituality: thoughts and insights, questions for reflection (and conversation), and suggestions for things to do. We begin by looking at the reality of spirituality, with a few of its foundations and characteristics, then moving to some unique ways that spirituality is fostered and lived in our lives as catechists. In the words of the poet Mary Oliver regarding ways to live life: "Pay attention. Be astonished. Tell about it."

Janet Schaeffler, OP

What is spirituality?

Have you ever found yourself thinking that "spirituality" is not really a part of your life, that it's something for someone else? Or do you sometimes view spirituality as only a part of your life, the part reserved for prayer, liturgy, Scripture reading, and other religious practices? These practices of prayer (and many more) are certainly an integral and indispensable part of spirituality, but is spirituality more than prayer life, more than spiritual practices?

We might view these practices as habits that help us step away for a while from the rest of our lives, to "escape" from the parts of our lives that aren't "spiritual." We may even view the "worldly" parts of our life as decadent, as unholy. What, then, is spirituality? The following story might provide some insights.

The monks in an ancient monastery were losing their spirit, becoming ornery and irritable with one another. The abbot sought the guidance of a wise rabbi, who responded, "I have no advice. The only thing I can tell you is that the Messiah is among you." The abbot conveyed this message to his fellow monks, adding, "I don't know what he meant." The monks began to ponder: Did he mean the Messiah is here, one of us? Who could it be? The abbot who has led us? Brother James, who is always late, yet exudes kindness? Brother Richard, who is so passive, yet always appears when help is needed? Of course, each monk said to himself, the hermit didn't mean me; I'm just an ordinary person.

With these thoughts running through their minds, the monks began to treat each other with exceptional reverence, kindness, and care on the off chance that one among them might be the Messiah. Because there was the possibility that each monk himself might be the Messiah, they began to regard themselves with extraordinary respect too.

"The Messiah is among you." There is no limit to the presence of God with us; therefore, everyone, every occurrence, everything is a part of our spirituality.

The Old Testament reminds us: "Where can I go from your spirit? From your presence, where can I flee?" No matter where the psalmist envisions, he realizes "even there your hand guides me, your right hand holds me fast" (Psalm 139:7-10).

In the New Testament, Jesus says to us: "I am with you always, until the end of the age" (Matthew 28:20).

Spirituality encompasses everything about us. Spirituality is holistic and integrated within the totality of our lives. Because Jesus became incarnate, became one of us, every ounce of creation is holy. Everything is held close in God's gracious embrace.

Every dimension of our lives is touched by our spirituality:

- our worries and concerns about the future
- the ways we respond to the needy in our midst
- the busyness of today's life
- the disappointments and challenges of life
- grieving the loss of a loved one
- the joy of birth and new life
- living faithfully the single life

- our interactions and interconnectedness with family, relatives, friends, coworkers
- the struggle of living with illness
- navigating congested traffic
- living as a faithful citizen
- integrating our sexuality
- caring for others and for the beauty of creation
- making decisions—the simple ones and the complex ones
- the delight of celebration times, etc.

During an interview with Krista Tippett on her radio show, "On Being," Sylvia Boorstein remarked, "Spirituality doesn't look like sitting down and meditating. Spirituality looks like folding the towels in a sweet way and talking kindly to the people in the family even though you've had a long day. It's enfolded into the act of parenting. You fold the towels in a sweet way. It doesn't take extra time."

A DEFINITION OF SPIRITUALITY

There are numerous (in reality, unlimited) definitions of spirituality. What a gift this is, because each definition helps us to understand and appreciate this mystery in a distinct way.

Years ago, I heard one description of spirituality that resonates with the reality that spirituality encompasses the totality of our lives: "Spirituality is who we are and what we do because of what we believe." There is nothing left out of our spirituality. The way we live our spirituality is influenced by our worldview, by the beliefs we hold dear, by the beliefs that have become a part of our lives.

Over the years as I've reflected upon that definition, I have added another component: "Spirituality is who we are and what we do because of what we believe and because of what we've experienced."

Our beliefs don't just happen. Our beliefs are a result of our experiences. What have you experienced that has formed your beliefs? Probably many things, but one of the core experiences that influences our beliefs (and all that we are) is our experience of God. Not simply our *knowledge about* God, but our *experience of* God.

- When have you realized—and experienced—God's lavish love?
- When have you been touched by—experienced—God's gentle care?
- When have you wondered at—and experienced—God's imaginative creativity?
- When have you appreciated—and experienced—God's unconditional acceptance?
- When have you been nudged by—experienced—God's disquieting challenge?

Our study, reflection, and conversations have told us *about* God. When and where in our daily lives have we *experienced* the God that we know about? These experiences of God deepen who we are. These experiences form our beliefs, which then impact all that we are, all that we do.

At times, some people might say they haven't or don't experience God. Perhaps it's not that we haven't, but, rather, that we aren't aware of the times and ways we have! Our lives can get so crowded and busy that we don't give ourselves time to be aware, to experience the closeness of our God. One of our roles as catechists, while deepening God-awareness in our own lives, is to walk with people, encouraging and empowering them to become attuned to the experience of God in their lives.

A DIVERSITY OF SPIRITUALITIES

People often speak of differences in spirituality related to who we are and our life stages (lay spirituality, married spirituality, the spirituality of the single person, spirituality in or of the workplace, etc.). Throughout the centuries, we have realized that there are also various expressions of spirituality flowing from some of our great saints and religious orders (Dominican, Franciscan, Benedictine, Augustinian, Jesuit, Carmelite, to name a few). We also recognize that there are distinctive spiritualities within various cultures (Celtic spirituality, Hispanic spirituality, Native American spirituality, etc.). Diverse spiritualities can also be witnessed in various movements or groups within today's church (Charismatic spirituality, Cursillo spirituality, etc.).

Each of these spiritualities is unique, but that does not mean that they are contradictory. They all arise from the same rich heritage of Christianity; they all aim at the same goal: to live and love as Jesus did. The difference is a matter of emphasis. Within the various spiritualities, each focuses on specific, and often different, elements of living discipleship, for instance:

- hospitality
- seeing God in all things
- commitment to the poor
- contemplation in action
- devotion to truth
- living simply
- living and promoting community
- prophetic signs in the world
- living and bringing compassion to the world

YOUR SPIRITUALITY INITIALS

As we look at the spiritualities flowing from some of the saints and religious orders throughout history, we find initials after the names of people who belong to these religious communities: O.P. for Dominicans (Order of Preachers), S.J. for Jesuits (Society of Jesus), O.S.B. for Benedictines (Order of Saint Benedict), etc. The initials tell us that the spirituality of these individuals has been formed in large part by the spirituality of their founder and the spirituality of their community.

In reality, each of us has spirituality initials. You might be a H.F.C. (Husband, Father, Caregiver). Perhaps you are an A.D.T. (Aunt, Dreamer, Teacher). Your initials might be C-C.F. (Creation-centered Friend) or P.G.C. (Protector, Grandparent, Catechist). What are your spirituality initials, especially at this point in your life?

To determine your unique spirituality initials, take time to consider the people and experiences that have formed you throughout your life. What roles in your life are currently forming who you are? What has helped you realize that there is more to life than meets the eye?

Since all the experiences of our lives form our spirituality, our growth in spirituality is never-ending. A few years from now, because of changing experiences and roles in life, your spirituality initials might be very different from today.

SPIRITUALITY: CONTINUALLY COMING HOME

Spirituality is the journey of coming home, of being home, of being one with our amazing God. Years ago when I was on Mackinac Island (between the upper and lower peninsulas of Michigan), a guide told us that no deer had ever resided there. One summer, several deer were brought over because people thought their presence might enhance this charming island.

But the following winter, when Lake Huron froze, the deer left the island and traveled back across the ice to the lower peninsula. They knew where home was; they needed to be rooted in home. Our journey of spirituality roots us where we need to be—at home with our God.

SPIRITUALITY OF CATECHISTS

Flowing from these realities—the various expressions of spirituality in our tradition as well as our own formative experiences—we can ask the question: might there be a unique spirituality for catechists?

The gift and responsibility of being called to be a catechist enhance our experiences and help to form our beliefs and practices. Our ministry as catechists influences who we are and what we do, while, at the same time, calling and enabling us to grow in spirituality, probably in unique ways, ways we might never experience if we weren't catechists.

Spirituality can be considered from various viewpoints. Three aspects (among many) are foundational to all spirituality, empowering us to live as disciples day in and day out. These three aspects also energize the spirituality and ministry of who we are as catechists. (We will also continue to explore additional facets of these three aspects in the chapters to come.)

*1. **Our own experiences of the paschal mystery:*** The life, death, and resurrection of Jesus was not something that happened only to Jesus. Jesus lived and experienced human life, suffered, and was raised to life because that is the life to which we are called: a life of human experience and relationships, sufferings, disappointments, losses, and grief, as well as the experience of peace-filled new beginnings, dreams, joys, precious moments, and glorious new life. God, through the resurrected

Christ and the Holy Spirit, is always with us throughout our journey of the paschal mystery.

As catechists, being ourselves rooted in this life of Jesus, we walk with others in their paschal mystery of life, supporting and guiding.

2. ***Letting God love us:*** We are called to serve, to wash feet. God reaches out to wash our feet first, to love us as we are. Created in the image and likeness of God, we are good. That is how God sees us, inviting us to believe in our goodness.

As catechists, because of our compassionate loving and service to others, adults, youth, and children experience God's love for them in a distinctive and tangible way.

3. ***Always more than me:*** It is difficult for the parts of a whole to fulfill the vision, the purpose, of the whole. One can't do it alone. We're always in this together. There is an African proverb that says, "Ubuntu. I am because we are." Your fears are mine; your searching and dreams are mine; our yearnings are common. The spirituality of each of us grows, thrives, and serves because we live it together.

As catechists, through our witnessing and teaching, we model unity for others, calling them to immerse themselves into the comfort and challenge of community.

Questions for reflection and discussion

- What is your definition of spirituality?
- When and where have you experienced God?

- What are your spirituality initials? Who and what have influenced you? What has formed and molded you? Who and what have helped you to experience God? Who and what have helped you to realize that there is more to life than what meets the eye?

- As you reflect on your experiences as a catechist, in what ways have you grown and changed?

- How does your spirituality influence who you are as a catechist?

Things to do

- Write down your spirituality initials. Periodically during prayer reflect on them. How do these facets of your life deepen your connection with God?

- Think about how your spirituality has changed over the years. Draw a timeline or a spiral, illustrating some of the changes.

- Decide upon a way to slow down so that you might be more aware of all the God-moments in your day.

- Make a plan for yourself. In what areas do you want to continue to grow? How will being a catechist help you?

- Each week choose a specific person to treat as though they were the Messiah. They are Christ among us, aren't they?

2

Some characteristics *of a* Catholic Christian spirituality

Everyone has a spirituality. Of course, the focus of spirituality will vary according to one's experiences, one's motivation for life and meaning, one's beliefs, and one's ever-deepening relationship with God.

As we explore spirituality (in its many manifestations), what are some characteristics that make it uniquely Catholic Christian? There are many; the beauty and gift of reflection on our experience (and the experiences of all in the Family of God, past and present) is that we become aware of more and more of these features. Let us explore just a few of the core characteristics of a Catholic Christian spirituality.

COMMUNAL

Our last chapter concluded with this important reality. It is such a profound characteristic that we begin with it again. Jesus' whole life was about community:

- Jesus gathered apostles with whom to share the building of the kingdom.
- Jesus ate with all kinds of people.
- Jesus modeled that the essence of life is how we interact with others.
- Jesus taught the Our Father, a prayer of a community rooted in forgiveness.
- Jesus sent the apostles forth to be with others: washing feet, bringing the Good News.

Prior to Jesus' example and life, from the very beginning of creation, God formed us and called us to community. All of creation is interdependent, woven together from mutual interconnections.

There are some belief systems that accentuate a me-and-God spirituality. Not us! An "individual Christian" is an oxymoron. A challenging characteristic of Christianity is that we are not called by God as individuals. We don't go to God alone. We go to God as a community, or we don't go.

One of the challenges of this characteristic is the inclusivity of community. Sometimes we think of community as like-minded people, those sharing the same beliefs, values, and goals. The ultimate challenge of community, taught and lived by Jesus, is that our community always needs to be expanded, always needs to widen the circle, so that eventually there will be no one outside the circle. A communal spirituality is all-encompassing, with no one left out.

In the New Testament we find the phrase "one another" or "each other" over fifty times. We hear the call to love one another, pray for each other, greet each other, teach each other, encourage each other, bear each other's burdens, serve each other, forgive each other, admonish each other, accept each other, be devoted to each other. Sometimes we might think that it is easier to live a life rooted in deep spirituality when no one else is around. That isn't the way God made us; that isn't the way God calls us.

Recently my niece asked her son, "Why do you think God made humans?" My seven-year-old great-nephew replied, "So that we could name the animals." Michelle said, 'That's right; I wonder if there is anything else?" Owen immediately answered, "Oh, yes. It's all about relationships."

Community and relationships, with God, with one another, with all creation, is a hallmark of Christian spirituality. In the words of Emily Green Balch, the 1946 Nobel Peace Laureate: "We have a long, long way to go. So let us hasten along the road, the road of human tenderness and generosity." Reaching out, "we may find one another's hands in the dark."

TRINITARIAN

Often we focus on the mystery of the Trinity once a year, on the feast of the Most Holy Trinity. Yet the Trinity is foundational to who we are and how we live. Joann Wolski Conn reminds us: "For Christians, it (spirituality) means one's entire life as understood, felt, imagined, and decided upon in relationship to God, in Christ Jesus, empowered by the Spirit" (*Spirituality and Personal Maturity*).

A Trinitarian focus returns us again to the characteristic of community, interdependence, and relationships. At times we think of the Trinity in terms of separate "roles." God the Father is Creator; God the Son is Redeemer; and God the Holy Spirit is Sanctifier. But understanding things from this perspective can place performance ahead of relationship (perhaps an expected response from our busy, need-to-be-organized, success-oriented world today).

In reality, God IS relationship. Even when we say, "God is Creator; God is Father," we're not talking about roles; we're not describing actions that God performs. It is much more than that. Rather, creating is what God is. Being redemptive, being the means by which life is given, is what God the Son is, not just something the Son does. Being consoler, inspirer, is what God the Holy Spirit is.

The Trinitarian God is the never-ending explosion of unfathomable love: bursting forth in creation, bursting forth in humanity, bursting forth as comforter and unifier, the ceaseless outpouring love and community in Father, in Son, and in Spirit. These are three ways in which God communicates what it is to be God. As we live a Trinitarian spirituality, we experience that these are the three ways in which God gives God's self to us. Or, to look at it from the other side, these are the ways I know I am thoroughly related to God.

Because God is unending and abundant relationship, I know who I am. Because the Trinity, by its very nature, is the relationship of love shared by the Father, Son, and Holy Spirit, it overflows. This God-love extends the possibility of intimate sharing between God and humans and, flowing from that, between all humans, among all humanity. We, too, are immersed in relationship.

Because of the Trinity, we know and experience the unconditional love of God. In turn, we love God, for that is how we are created—in God's image. Because God is all about relationship, our response of loving God is not like a bridge to God that we build because of our good actions, our prayer, and our virtuous way of life. Rather, God, who is love, has and will always love us; therefore, we love, we pray, and we live a holy life because we have been first loved.

Our love (as God's) can never stop or stay stagnant; our love (because we have been loved) overflows continually and constantly to all humanity, to all creation.

CHRIST-CENTERED

How are we able to know and experience this mystery of God, this mystery of the Trinity? It is apparent that Christian spirituality, by its very name as well as by the realization of who we are from the moment of our baptism, is a way of believing, experiencing, and living that is rooted in the person and vision of Jesus Christ.

It is through Jesus that seekers and believers come to know God, the mystery of the Trinity. Jesus is the image of the invisible God (Colossians 1:15).

Often I've heard people remark, "Jesus is the answer." To which we might each ask, "What is the question?" The question might be different for each one of us; yet this answer and all the possible questions point to the reality of the centrality of Jesus for who we are and whose we are. We realize that our spirituality is an encounter with the person of Jesus.

By meeting Christ, and choosing to follow him, we come to know who we are. Saint Augustine spoke of Christians as other Christs. One of the reasons he did this was because he understood the incarnation (God becoming human) as going beyond the birth of Jesus. Each and every one of us shares in the incarnation. We carry Christ in every aspect of our lives, 24/7.

SEEING THE SACRED IN THE ORDINARY

At times do we picture God as "up there," as an absentee landlord who, once in a while, comes to us? A Catholic Christian spirituality sees the reality of God's presence in another way: God did not set the universe in motion, retiring to heaven to watch it unfold. Rather, God is with us everywhere in our everyday lives of struggles and joys, questions and hopes, work and play, gratitude and questions, relationships and intimacy. God is there in our vocation of building the reign of God.

Our poets have continually reminded us of this. For example, in her poem "Aurora Leigh," Elizabeth Barrett Browning wrote that "Earth is crammed with heaven and every common bush afire with God." Gerard Manley Hopkins proclaimed: "Christ plays in ten thousand places..." ("As Kingfishers Catch Fire"), and "The world is charged with the grandeur of God..." ("God's Grandeur").

Our spirituality impels us to see God everywhere. We don't have compartmentalized lives. All is sacred because God permeates everything, when we have eyes to see. Our Catholic tradition has always affirmed this in what we call "the principle of sacramentality"—God is present to us, and we respond to God's grace through the ordinary and everydayness of our lives.

Saint Francis of Assisi tells this wonderful story:

> I once spoke to my friend, an old squirrel,
>   about the Sacraments -
> he got so excited and ran into a hollow in his tree
> and came back holding some acorns, an owl feather
> and a ribbon he found.
>
> And I just smiled and said, "Yes, dear, you understand
> everything imparts God's grace."

We know that we have been gifted with the seven sacraments—sacred symbols that mediate God's grace in an intensified way. Perhaps our celebrations of the sacraments have their deepest meaning when we first live lives of seeing and experiencing God everywhere.

Do we become enthralled with the ordinary things: the textures and colors of leaves, the smile from a stranger, the sound of soft rain, someone who asks you how you're really doing, the peaceful night darkness, listening to a three-year-old, the aroma of baking chocolate chip cookies, your favorite song?

In *The Last Temptation of Christ,* Nikos Kazantzakis imagines the following scene with Christ's words and the response of the people: "'Everything is a miracle...what further miracles do you want? Look below you: even the humblest blade of grass has its guardian angel who stands by and helps it to grow....And, if you close your eyes, what a miracle the world within us!'...The people listened to him, and the clay within them turned into wings....if you lifted a stone you found God underneath, if you knocked on a door, God came out to open it for you..."

Fr. Anthony deMello reminds us: "We forget all too easily that one of the big lessons of the Incarnation is that God is found in the ordinary. You wish to see God? Look at the face of the man next to you. You want to hear him? Listen to the cry of a baby, the loud laughter at a party, the wind rustling in the trees. You want to feel him? Stretch your hand out and hold someone. Or touch the chair you are sitting on or this book that you are reading. Or just quiet yourself, become aware of the sensations in your body, sense his almighty power at work in you and feel how near he is to you. Emmanuel, God-with-us."

SEEING WITH GOD'S EYES

This characteristic flows from the principle of sacramentality. As many of the gospel passages remind us, are we "blind" or are we ready to open our eyes and see things in new ways, in ways that God sees: seeing the goodness and expecting the best?

Can we act as though we are tourists in our everyday world: watching for the magnificent, in small things as well as big things; growing in appreciation for all the goodness around us?

Seeing with God's eyes empowers us to live a life of radical appreciation and respect for each individual, seeing their goodness, as this ancient story reminds us:

> A long time ago a traveler, seeking a place to live, came to a village. On the outskirts of this village sat an old man.
>
> "Old man," inquired the visitor, "what manner of people dwell here?" The old man replied with a question: "What were they like where you come from?"
>
> "The people were unkind, dishonest, prone to gossip, and unfriendly," said the visitor. "Well," returned the old man. "You will find that the residents of this village possess similar qualities. It may be wiser for you to continue your search for a place to live."
>
> Another wanderer, seeking a place to live, approached the same village and the same old man. Again the visitor asked him, "Sir, what manner of people dwell in yonder village?"
>
> And the old man repeated his question, "What were they like where you came from?"
>
> "The people were friendly, honest, fair, and willing to help a neighbor in need. I hope I have the good fortune to find such good people again," replied the visitor. "Be certain that you will discover such people as you have described in this village," said the wise old man.

Seeing with God's eyes enables us to understand and appreciate as God does: "God saw that it was good" (Genesis 1:10). Hildegard of Bingen, when meeting someone on the street, would recall: "Every creature is a glittering, glistening mirror of divinity."

There is an anonymous saying that reminds us how we strive to live when we see with God's eyes: "May I gaze at each person with a look that says I know so much good about you."

Once when I was going for a walk with my great-nephew Tyler, he abruptly stopped, bent down, and happily said, "Oh, my very favorite bug! Can I pet him?" Everything about creation was precious to Tyler.

Do we see, as Tyler did, with God's eyes, seeing the wholeness and beauty of God everywhere and always, even in the smallest of things, the simplest of happenings? Do we see everyone and everything imbued with exceptionality? What would happen if we cultivated an attitude of responding to everyone and everything with "Oh, my very favorite..."?

Seeing with God's eyes also invites us to see ourselves through God's eyes. Spend several minutes of quiet time each night quietly contemplating, gratefully celebrating, and perhaps reflectively writing in your journal about how God sees you when God looks at you—with wonder, love, and total acceptance.

As we see with God's eyes, we recognize God in each person, even—and especially—in the hurting and needy. *The Story of the Christmas Guest* by Helen Steiner Rice (also in a song by Reba McIntyre) tells us:

> Three times my shadow crossed your floor.
> Three times I came to your lowly door.
> I was the beggar with bruised cold feet;

I was the woman you gave something to eat;
I was the child on the homeless street.

Once when a catechist showed the children pictures of the Earth from space, a little girl asked, "Who drew the lines?"

"What do you mean?" the teacher asked.

The child said, "Look at these pictures. No lines. Look at the globe and maps. Lines. We drew the lines. God doesn't draw lines." Seeing with God's eyes eliminates all lines, all distinctions, all categories. Perhaps, especially as catechists, our spirituality is revealed in our eyes as we tenderly, attentively, and reverently recognize the presence of God in each person with whom we walk this journey of faith.

The poet Rilke once wrote of how he learned to stand "more seeingly" in front of certain paintings. Perhaps that is our call, especially as catechists: to stand before life, to stand before those to whom we minister, "more seeingly," seeing with God's eyes.

HOPE

"These are the best of times and the worst of times...an age of wisdom and an age of foolishness...it was the season of light, it was a season of darkness...it was the spring of hope and the winter of despair." These opening lines of Dickens's *A Tale of Two Cities* could be the modern telling of "There is an appointed time for everything, and a time for every purpose under the heavens: a time to weep and a time to laugh...a time to mourn and a time to dance; a time to seek and a time to lose..." (Ecclesiastes 3:1-8).

In all of these times, we are called to be people of hope. What a needed characteristic of Catholic Christian spirituality! Physicians tell us that the human body can survive four to six weeks without food, up to three days without water, and for about ten minutes without oxygen. We know, from our experience, that living without hope takes a toll, a death-toll, on our human spirits.

Hope infuses life with peace; it opens our hearts to others, and our minds to future possibilities. Hope is rooted in faith; it colors faith with kindness and perseverance. Hope reminds us that creation continues, that we are still comprehending the significance of Jesus' life, death, and resurrection, that all of God's dreams are yet to be known. Hope continually stirs within us, telling us that "eye has not seen, and ear has not heard...what God has prepared for those who love God" (1 Corinthians 2:9).

Hope-filled people experience as many frustrations and disappointments as anyone else; they're just better equipped to withstand them and thus hang in there for the long haul. We hope because of the promises we have been given. We hope because we have experienced God.

In the homily during his installation Mass, Pope Francis prompted us with these words: "Today amid so much darkness we need to see the light of hope and to be men and women who bring hope to others. To protect creation, to protect every man and every woman, to look upon them with tenderness and love, is to open up a horizon of hope; it is to let a shaft of light break through the heavy clouds."

Pierre Teilhard de Chardin said: "The future belongs to those who give the next generation reason for hope." What a challenge, what a privilege for us as disciples, for us as catechists!

COMPASSIONATE RESPONSE

The virtue of hope brings us to this trait. Hope compels us to take responsibility for the future. God created the universe as a developing organism, always growing, always moving beyond, ahead, and forward. This call to build the kingdom—here and hereafter—requires us to be compassionate people, always reaching out in justice and peace-making.

Many times, as we think (and talk) about spirituality, we presume a word before spirituality: "my." We can become proud of our spirituality: the ways we have chosen to pray, to meditate, to follow mentors who have lived holy lives. Yet everything in the Catholic tradition (and other traditions) stresses the importance of a life with and for others. The challenge of Jesus is not just to be a good person but to live and act so that our lives touch everyone, touch the needs of today, and work for the good of humanity.

Spirituality is not just between me and God. For the Old Testament prophets, the test of faith was not how we "feel" about God, but our response to the question, "How are the poor doing in my area?" Have you ever prayed with the daily newspaper (or internet news) in one hand and with Scripture in the other? Would that call you to do something right here and right now?

Catholic Christians do more than reflect on their own internal growth; they are active. They write letters; they reach out to the grieving in their neighborhoods; they work in soup kitchens; they organize neighbors to buy from local farmers; they call family members and friends who are lonely; they read to the blind; they respond when someone in need interrupts their plans for their day.

It's a breath-taking reality that often those who are hurting most somehow know and find the strength to reach out to others in compassion, in service. When my six-year-old great-nephew died suddenly, my niece and her husband, and my sister and brother-in-law, amid their heart-wrenching grief, took time for others: walking with others who experienced the death of a child, and becoming involved in groups and endeavors that responded to the suffering needs of others.

Questions for reflection and discussion

- If someone were to watch you closely for one week, what might that person think are the characteristics that guide your life?
- Which manifestation of God do you usually think about, relate to—the Father, the Son, or the Holy Spirit? Why do you think that is so?
- "Jesus is the answer." What would your question be?
- When you see with God's eyes, what is apparent to you?
- Who is a person of hope for you? Who touches your life with hope? To whom do you go to find hope? What brings you the most hope these days?

Things to do

- Is there someone who is not "in" your community right now? Decide on one action you could do in the next several weeks to widen your circle.
- Write in your journal each evening two ways you experi-

enced God in the ordinary that day or one way you saw with God's eyes during that day.

- Pearl Bailey said, "People see God every day; they just don't recognize him!" Be aware of your everyday moments: where is God in them? Do you find God in the noisy crowd or in church—or both?

- Collect some stories of hope. Share hope-filled stories with others.

- Place a picture of the Earth on your dinner table or as your computer screensaver. Talk with a friend, a family member, or those to whom you minister in catechetics, about ways to eliminate the lines we draw.

The universal call *to* holiness

A few years ago there was a nationwide telephone survey of a thousand people on the topic of holiness (conducted by the Barna Group). Some of the results were:

- Three out of every four persons (73%) believe that it is possible for someone to become holy, regardless of their past.
- Only half (50%) said that they know someone they consider to be holy.
- That's more than twice as many who consider themselves to be holy (21%).
- When asked to describe what it means to be holy, the adults gave a wide range of answers. The most common reply: I don't know (20%). Other responses fell into such categories as: being Christlike (19%); making faith your top priority in life (18%); having a good attitude about people and life (10%); and being guided by the Holy Spirit (9%).

(How would you have responded to the questions?)

HOLINESS: ALL ARE CALLED

You might remember an illustration in the *Baltimore Catechism*. Under a picture of a couple getting married, it said: "This is good." Immediately next to it, there was a photo of a nun praying, with the caption: "This is better."

One of the many ways in which the Second Vatican Council (1962-1965) returned us to the beliefs and practices of the early church was to ardently reverse this thinking, based upon and rediscovering the teachings of Scripture:

> For all of you who were baptized into Christ have clothed yourselves with Christ. There is neither Jew nor Greek, there is neither slave nor free person, there is not male and female; for you are all one in Christ Jesus. (Galatians 3:27-28)

> So be perfect, just as your heavenly Father is perfect. (Matthew 5:48)

> But you are "a chosen race, a royal priesthood, a holy nation, a people of his own, so that you may announce the praises" of him who called you out of darkness into his wonderful light. (1 Peter 2:9)

Everyone, without distinction, is called to holiness.

The documents of the Second Vatican Council over and over again remind us that the call to holiness is for everyone. Chapter Five of *Lumen Gentium*, the Dogmatic Constitution on the Church, defines the goal of human life as holiness, the first time a church document had said such a thing.

> It is evident to everyone that all the faithful of Christ of whatever rank or status are called to the fullness of the Christian life and to the perfection of charity. (*LG*, #40)

> In the various types and duties of life, one and the same holiness is cultivated by all who are moved by the Spirit of God... (*LG*, #41)

HOLINESS THROUGHOUT OUR HISTORY

All are called to holiness; there aren't certain members of the church who are holier simply because of their state in life. The Second Vatican Council did not invent this concept. The Council was reminding the faithful of the teachings of Scripture and the practices of the early church. No church document had previously talked about the universal call to holiness, but Scripture is filled with messages about this gift, making no distinctions, calling all to one holiness:

> Sanctify yourselves, then, and be holy; for I, the Lord, your God, am holy. (Leviticus 20:7)

> As he who called you is holy, be holy yourselves in every aspect of your conduct, for it is written, "Be holy because I (am) holy." (1 Peter 1:15-16)

> Strive for peace with everyone, and for that holiness without which no one will see the Lord. (Hebrews 12:14)

> This is the will of God, your holiness... (1 Thessalonians 4:3)

WHAT IS HOLINESS?

We are called to holiness; it is our response to God, who first loved us. We have a responsibility for our growth in holiness. But the responsibility doesn't all rest on us; it's not all about us. We are holy because that's how God made us; we are made in the image and likeness of God. The work of the Holy Spirit helps us intensify that reality: sanctifying us, deepening our holiness.

Holiness is not a reward that we earn; it's not, ultimately, something that we do. God has made us holy. Of course, we respond. Holiness is not a gift, a reward that comes after we have been willing to live a life of service to others; we care and serve others because we are holy.

Holiness does not come because we pray; we want to pray because we are holy. Holiness is not a result of being and doing good; we are good; we do good because we are holy.

In an October 1998 article in *U.S. Catholic*, Father Robert Barron recounts a conversation he had with Father Godfrey Diekmann, OSB, one of the leaders of the liturgical movement in the United States and a major contributor to shaping Vatican II's document on the liturgy.

Father Barron asked: "Godfrey, if you were young again and you could mount the barricades, what would you speak out for today in the church?"

Fr. Diekmann replied, "Deification." He went on to explain that in the 1930s he listened to the lectures of Karl Adam. "He told us that we start at the top, that we start as children of God. The essence of the spiritual life is not trying to make ourselves worthy of God because God has already made us worthy. The essence of the spiritual life is to live out the implications of our dignity as deified children of the Father. That's what I'd fight for. That's what I'd tell the people."

In 2 Peter 1:4 we hear: "Through these promises you may become partakers of the divine nature." Saint Athanasius, in teaching about the purpose of the Incarnation, said: "God became man (human) that we might be made God." This concept of deification is found in the *Catechism of the Catholic Church* (#460, 1129, 1265, 1812, 1988, and 1999). Section #1988 reminds us: "[God} gave Himself to us through His Spirit. By participation of the Spirit, we become communicants in the divine nature... For this reason, those in whom the Spirit dwells are divinized."

This reality is also found in the *United States Catholic Catechism for Adults* (pages 41, 79, 80, 87, 93, 193, 328, and 329). This reality of deification, then, is another way of understanding our call to holiness; we are holy as God is holy because we are created in the image of God.

HOLINESS LIVED EVERY DAY

How, where, and when do we actually live this call to holiness? Pause for a moment and think about the various roles you have in life. In addition to being a catechist, are you a spouse, a parent, a daughter or son, a sister or brother, an aunt or uncle, a cousin, an accountant, a teacher, a plumber, a nurse or doctor, an administrative assistant, a computer programmer, a sales clerk, a caregiver, a eucharistic minister, lector, usher or cantor, a member of your parish pastoral council or parish commissions, a board member, a library (or other) volunteer, etc.?

All of these various roles (and all those you haven't thought of yet), which are many ways of being human, are your path to holiness. Sometimes we have a distorted sense of holiness; at times people think that holiness "happens" only in church or at times of prayer, that holiness is just a little bit different than being human.

Being human is the way we become holy. Being human is

the way God made us, and God thought it was very good. Our path to holiness is not just going to church (as important as that is). The time we spend in church might be about 3 or 4% of our lives; it's not the only part. Our path to holiness is in the everydayness of our human lives. That's where we find God and our call to holiness.

In *The Color Purple*, Shug has a strong belief that God is a part of everything. One day she says: "Celie, tell the truth, have you ever found God in church? I never did. I just found a bunch of folks hoping for him to show. Any God I ever felt in church I brought in with me. And I think all the other folks did too. They come to church to share God, not find God."

If that is the reality, where do we find God? Where is God? We find God—we experience God—in our everyday lives. At times that is our challenge: constantly remembering that God is always with us, sometimes much more than we can imagine. Somehow, at times, we think we have to find God and then put God into our lives. God, however, is already there. Our task is to slow down, taking the time to realize the holiness of our daily lives, the holiness of being and living humanity, taking time to experience God in the ordinariness of our lives.

God is in the everyday; that is where holiness is deepened; holiness is lived through all that we do in our everyday lives. Sometimes I think God and we are like two children playing hide-'n'-go-seek. God decides to hide; at some point(s), we decide not to play. God hides in the ordinary things, in the usual events of our daily lives. If we don't look there, imagine how God feels.

God comes to us in the everydayness of our lives; that is where we live our holiness. That's where we are already holy. We are holy when we take time to care for our spouse or children when we'd rather do the things on our agenda. We are holy when we call our lonely neighbor and invite him or her for dinner when we'd rather go out to dinner by ourselves. We are holy when we decide not to gossip even though everyone else finds it easy to do.

We become truly holy by being people of integrity and compassion in our friendships, our parenting, our marriage, our work, and in our search for peace, truth, and justice in our world. Karl Rahner, a twentieth-century theologian, maintained that the most comprehensive task of a Christian is to become human—a human person (like Jesus) whose roots are divine.

Sometimes we talk about adding things into our lives and giving things up so that we might become holier. Even though, at times, that might be true, most often we probably don't need to do that. Reflect on some of the things that are already in our days: the challenges, the disruptions that come when we think we have our day planned, the inevitable disappointments and discouragements, the requests for help that come from our family, friends, and acquaintances, the needs of our world. When we respond to these (and others) with unconditional love, caring, forgiveness, compassion, and service, we probably have all we need to live our holiness.

In a 1980 document, *Called and Gifted: The American Catholic Laity* (which flows from the Vatican II document *Lumen Gentium),* the U.S. bishops speak of holiness within the everyday:

> "It is characteristic that lay men and women hear the call to holiness in the very web of their existence (LG, #31), in and through the events of the world, the pluralism of modern living, the complex decisions and conflicting values they must struggle with, the richness and fragility of

> sexual relationships, the delicate balance between activity and stillness, presence and privacy, love and loss."

This touches upon some of the very real ways of living our everyday holiness.

Holiness is deepened when we jump into life with both feet, when we deal honestly and courageously with the inescapable events of everyday life, when through prayer we strive to see God present in all these events, supporting us, calling us to be precisely what we were created to be: good human persons.

How holiness is lived out, of course, is a little different for each person, for that is how God made us: unique individuals.

Questions for reflection and discussion

- Have you heard before this idea of everyone being called to holiness? Do you hear or have you heard it often? When? Where? How?
- If someone said about you, "____ is holy," how would that make you feel? Why do you think they would say it?
- Has your understanding of holiness changed over the course of your life? How?
- Who is a model of holiness for you?
- In your everyday life, when are you aware of God?

Things to do

- Look for books to read that share how others have lived, or are living, holiness in their everyday world.
- Be alert each day to people around you, people who are exuding holiness.
- Write down your definition of holiness. Check it in six months; has it changed?
- At the end of each day, jot down three ways that you lived your holiness—that you lived the core of who you are, the essence of whose you are.
- Decide on one thing you will do to deepen your living of holiness in the weeks to come.

4

Our image *of* God: An influence *on* our spirituality

There are many things that impact the spirituality that each of us lives. Perhaps one of the most formative influences is our image of God.

In fact, our image of, and our names for, God influence all that we are:

- Who our God is tells us who we are and how we are called to act
- What we think about God influences how we treat other people
- How we see God influences how we pray— individually and as a community

SOME REALITIES TO KEEP US ROOTED

As we reflect on how we see, image, and understand God, these following realities can keep us anchored.

God is a mystery. God is always beyond us. There is a legend that one day Saint Augustine walked along the Mediterranean shore, puzzling over some point he was writing about God. He half-watched a small child going back and forth from the water's edge, repeatedly filling a pail, pouring the water into a hole dug in the sand. Augustine finally asked what he was doing. The young child replied, "Trying to put the sea into my hole."

"You can't do that. It won't fit," answered Augustine. The child replied, "Neither can you put the mystery of God into your mind; it won't fit."

As Margaret Silf explains in *The Gift of Prayer,* "God is always going to be bigger than any image we can form. If it were not so, God would not be God. The mystery is always going to lie beyond our rational comprehension..."

All images (and titles/names) say something about who God is and what God is like, but never the total reality. Is God really a father? Is God like a father? Is God really fire? Is God like fire?

As humans, we use countless words, many names, diverse images, and meaningful symbols to describe our various understandings of our experiences. When it comes to our awareness and experience of God, it is a little different. God is beyond our images and ideas. Fortunately, we have wonderful and varied names, images, and symbols for God. Yet all of our human statements about God are never actual and complete descriptions of God. At the same time, when we are able to explore a variety of images and metaphors, it frees us to examine many different ways of understanding who God is.

When we want to talk about God, Saint Thomas Aquinas cautions us that "we cannot say what God is"; we can say only "what God is not."

No expression of God can be taken literally. Our language is like a finger pointing to the moon, not the moon itself. We can only speak of God by using images, metaphors, and analogies. Scripture gifts us with many images for God. We could view them through five different categories:

- God images from personal relationships: father, mother, husband, female beloved, companion, bridegroom, friend, suffering servant, protector
- God images from political life: advocate, liberator, king, warrior, judge, lawgiver
- God images from a wide array of human crafts and professions: good shepherd, dairymaid, farmer, laundress, construction worker, potter, sower of good seed, fisherman, midwife, merchant, physician, bakerwoman, gardener, healer, teacher, writer, artist, nurse, metal worker, homemaker, woman giving birth, woman nursing her young, mother dedicated to child care
- God images taken from the animal kingdom: roaring lion, hovering mother bird, angry mother bear, protective mother hen, eagle
- God images from cosmic reality: light, cloud, rock, fire, wind, mountaintop, living water, refreshing water, life itself

These images are wide and varied (and there's many, many more in our tradition and in other traditions). Yet nothing that we say about God can claim to be the complete truth. God transcends our human experience.

From looking at history, we "see the necessity of giving to God many names," says Saint Thomas Aquinas. If we were capable of expressing the fullness of God in one complete name, the proliferation of names, images, and concepts that we see throughout the history of religions would make no sense at all.

But there is no one such name. Rather, human beings name God with a symphony of names. What a gift that is! (This reality is beautifully illustrated in the children's book *Old Turtle* by Douglas Wood.)

As we focus on Scripture and our tradition, we see the multitude of names and images. Even taking all the names and images that have been used throughout history and putting them completely together never gives the whole picture. Saint Augustine reminds us: "If you have understood, it is not God."

God is more than we could ever imagine. Recently, at the time of the Super Bowl, a large group of people was asked whether they pray for a specific team to win. One young child was asked, "Does God care about the Super Bowl?" He immediately replied, "No, God is big!"

It is even challenging for us to imagine God's love for us since it is so much more than any human is capable of. Think of your wonder and gratitude for the love of the person who loves you the most; realize that is miniscule compared to the love of God for you. Yet, when we are aware, even in our limited way, of God's overwhelming love for us, it changes everything. Pedro Arrupe, the Superior General of the Jesuits from 1965-1983, summarized it this way:

> "Nothing is more practical than finding God, that is, than falling in love in a quite absolute, final way. What you are in love with, what seizes your imagination, will affect everything. It will decide what will get you out of bed in the morning, what

> you do with your evenings, how you spend your weekends, what you read, whom you know, what breaks your heart, and what amazes you with joy and gratitude. Fall in love, stay in love, and it will decide everything."

God is ever-present; we don't control God's presence with us. Because of God's very nature of love, God is always with us. God is closer to us than we could ever imagine. If we ever feel that God is far away, guess who moved?

Yet, at times, how do we pray? Is our image of God one that prompts us to ask God to come and be with us? If God is within us, around us, enfolding us in love and grace all the time, do we need to pray that way? Perhaps our prayer needs to be one of quieting, one of asking the Holy Spirit to calm us down, to make us more aware of the unceasing nearness of God's presence and love that is already—and always—with us.

SOME CHALLENGES FOR US

Reflecting on our images and names for God also raises some challenges for us.

Are our images of God always growing? Do we have the same names/images, the same experiences of God, that we had when we were children, fifteen years ago, last year?

As faith-filled disciples, our understanding of God—and, most importantly, our relationship with God—is always changing. Fr. Albert Hasse, in *Swimming in the Sun: Discovering the Lord's Prayer with Francis of Assisi and Thomas Aquinas*, said:

> "We outgrow our images of God like we do our clothes and shoes. If we do not continually refine

> and update them as a result of our personal experiences of God, we run the risk of dreadful God-images, a childish spirituality, or even worse, the radical disbelief of atheism or agnosticism. The closer we get back home through asceticism, the better sight we have of the God waiting for us."

Thus, we need to be awake to our new experiences, to all that is happening in our lives, to all the ways God is present to us. Fr. Richard Rohr challenges us: "The greatest obstacle to a new experience of God is our last experience of God."

There are many faces of God, because each of us is a face of God. If we were to attempt to put together a listing of all the names, all the images for God that have been used throughout history, this list would be minimal compared to the number of people each of us will meet in our lifetimes, compared to the number of people in our world.

Each person is a face of God: with their gifts and liabilities, with their joys and fears, with their awe-inspiring, but sometimes feared, diversity. This powerful challenge calls for great openness on our part—openness to all people, openness to all cultures. Each and every person has the potential to reflect God to us.

Who our God is tells us who we are. Who our God is influences how we pray; who our God is impacts how we view church and envision the world. Most importantly, we become and we act like the image of God that we have.

Think for a moment about your favorite image, your favorite name, for God. Does that name or image also say anything about you? Do you act like that in your life? When? How?

Let's imagine a person whose predominant image of God is as Judge. Might that be how this person relates to others—evaluating their actions, judging their motives, being critical of both who they are and their responses to life?

Imagine another person who might have an image of God as the Loyal One, the Friend who stands by them, no matter what. Might that also be a description of how they act in all the areas of their lives: in their relationships with their family, their friends, their coworkers, those with whom they walk on the journey of faith as a catechist? Do they respond to all in their lives as friend, as the loyal one?

Questions for reflection and discussion

- When you pray or meditate, what is the image of God in your thoughts, your feelings? How did you come to this image of God?
- Who has been an image of God for you within the last few weeks?
- What kind of image of God have you been for others, for those you walk with in your ministry as catechist?
- Think of a favorite image (name) that you have for God. Does that say something about you? Do you act like this in your life?
- Orest Bedrij (scientist, businessman and mystic) said: "To know God without being Godlike is like trying to swim without entering water." How are you Godlike?

Things to do

- Use an art form (painting, clay, drawing, etc.) to form a symbol that says something to you about your image of God.

- Begin a list—in your journal, a page on your refrigerator door, etc.—of all the names and images of God that you know. What do you realize?

- "Listen" to your prayers. What do they tell you about your image of God?

- Find a photograph that you or a friend or family member has taken, or take a new one. What does it tell you about God?

- Edward Hays said, "Being extravagantly generous is an enchanting way to become holy and Godlike, for God is awesomely extravagant—as is revealed by even a casual glance at creation." Decide on one way you can be extravagant (like God).

5

Who are we *as* catechists?

One of the gifts (and challenges) of being a catechist is that we are called to many roles; there are various ways of describing who we are.

Often, young children can only see and understand a person in one way. When he was a little child, my nephew had a hard time comprehending that I could be both his aunt and his mom's sister. He was adamant about telling me that this couldn't be so.

We realize, though, what a privilege it is to be able to describe who we are from several viewpoints.

CATECHISTS: PEOPLE WHO ARE CALLED

God continually says to us, "I have called you by name: you are mine." Within that constant, affirming call is always an invitation—a challenge—to be who we are, whose we are, to use our gifts for others.

Probably for each of us, as we think about our beginnings in the catechetical ministry, we realize that we didn't explicitly choose this ministry; we were called. The invitation ultimately came from God. It might have been mediated through the director of adult faith formation, the pastor, a friend, the director of religious education, the coordinator of RCIA, another parishioner, the coordinator of the baptism program, or through the feelings and promptings of God in our hearts.

This call is an invitation to uniquely live our baptismal vocation. Even though the call might have been mediated through another, it is our unique call. We aren't merely "helping Father" or "assisting the director/coordinator"; we have uniquely been called by God because of our baptism, because of our gifts.

There might have been times—at the beginning, and even throughout the years—when we wondered about what we were really doing, why we said yes, and if we were really competent enough to do this. There's a saying reminding us that "God doesn't call the qualified; God qualifies the called."

Because this is a call, a vocation, when we do our part (e.g., our ongoing formation, development of both catechetical skills and love and respect for the learners), we know we are doing God's work. Responding to the call, we use our gifts and our committed faith for the good of others. The theologian Frederick Buechner challenges us: "The place God calls you to is the place where your deep gladness and the world's deep hunger meet."

Because this call from God is for the service of the community, the call is also from the church. We don't respond to the call or minister as individuals. We are ministering in God's name. We are ministering in the name of the faith-filled community, the church.

What support, empowerment, and challenge that gives us! We are surrounded by the wisdom, example, and commitment of the church throughout the world; we stand on the shoulders of those who came before us, sharing the Good News: the first disciples, Mary Magdalene, Paul, the early mothers and fathers of the church, Augustine and his mother Monica, Dominic, Thomas Aquinas, Catherine of Siena, Francis and Clare of Assisi, Charles Borromeo, Robert Bellarmine, Elizabeth Ann Seton, John Neumann, and Katharine Drexel, to name just a few.

CATECHISTS: PEOPLE LIVING THE MISSION

When Jesus was found in the temple, his response to Mary and Joseph was "I must be about my Father's business." Jesus realized and probably continued to grow into his mission—his Father's mission.

In his interviews for his book *Working,* Studs Terkel heard someone say, "I believe that most of us are looking for a calling, not a job." Scripture and our tradition speak of this calling as mission, the work of God that we are called to share. As catechists we are part of something much bigger than ourselves, much bigger than our individual parish: we participate in the mission of Jesus.

As Jesus grew and became a teacher, he was possibly discouraged at times. Among his learners there were those who didn't get it, those who expected preferential treatment, and those who were afraid. Through everything, Jesus persevered. He knew he was sent by God; he had a mission. Sharing in that mission, we are always surrounded by God's strength even and especially in the discouraging times.

CATECHISTS: PLANTERS OF SEEDS

We are called to mission, to be co-creators with God, but that doesn't mean we have to do everything. It is God's work; we do all we can, knowing that the grace of God and the support of community are at work in the hearts and lives of our adults, youth, and children.

The following was written in November 1979 by Bishop

(then Father) Ken Untener for a homily to be given by John Cardinal Dearden of Detroit. It vividly reminds us of our role of planting seeds—not doing everything, but that is all right.

> We accomplish in our lifetime only a tiny fraction
> of the magnificent enterprise that is God's work.
> Nothing we do is complete, which is a way of saying
> that the kingdom always lies beyond us.
> No statement says all that could be said.
> No prayer fully expresses our faith.
> No program accomplishes the church's mission.
>
> This is what we are about.
> We plant the seeds that one day will grow.
> We water seeds already planted,
> knowing that they hold future promise.
>
> We cannot do everything, and there is a sense
> of liberation in realizing that.
> This enables us to do something,
> and to do it very well. It may be incomplete,
> but it is a beginning, a step along the way,
> an opportunity for the Lord's grace to enter
> and do the rest.

CATECHISTS: COMPANIONS ON THE JOURNEY

The translation of "catechist" in some languages is "to grab a hand and walk along with." As the discouraged and sad disciples walked the road to Emmaus (Luke 24:13-35), Jesus joined them as a companion; Jesus shared life with them. Jesus grabbed their hands and walked with them.

On this Emmaus journey, Jesus, as a listener, as a fellow-traveler, as a companion, helped them to discover what they knew all along.

Companion comes from two Latin words, *cum* and *panis*, which mean "with" and "bread." As companions, catechists share bread with or walk the journey with others, recognizing that we're all on this journey together, and recognizing that, on this journey, all have something to give and all have something they need for continued growth.

Whether we minister with adults, youth, or children, our role is not to "put in," but to "call forth." An important definition of "education" is "to draw out of."

Catechists have the privilege of being companions—of walking with, of reawakening, and of calling forth what is already there. God is within those we serve; God is already present in their lives. As companions, we grab their hands and walk along with them, helping them to continually discover even more deeply the multiple ways of God's presence, God's unconditional love and strength with them.

CATECHISTS: PEOPLE OF WITNESS

Ralph Waldo Emerson said, "Who you are thunders at me so loudly, I can't hear what you are saying." Many years ago I heard the president of one of our publishing companies (which produce catechetical texts) say frequently, "Books don't teach people. People teach people."

We teach most profoundly (whether we know it or not) because of who we are, what we do, and the way we live. Leaders in all areas of education and formation remind us all the time that, as important as good techniques are, great teaching comes from who the teacher is, from the identity and integrity of the teacher.

One of the challenges of being a catechist might be that, at times, we don't know how to "measure" the impact, the learning, and the change in lives that happen in and for those with whom we walk on the journey of faith. Yet recall the times adults, youth, or children have said something like this to you (perhaps much later in their lives):

> Because you listened to me...
> Because you treated me with respect...
> Because I saw how you cared for the hurting...
> Because you shared with us your experience of God (of service, of hope, etc.)...
> Because of how you prayed with us...
> Because I saw your kindness with your family...
> ...my life was changed. Because of you I knew what Jesus was like.

More is caught than taught. We can't fool children—or adults! Who we are "teaches" and witnesses. Years ago, in *Fashion Me A People,* a landmark book that is still available today, Maria Harris wrote of three kinds of curriculum: explicit (what we say), implicit (what we do), and null (what we don't say, what we don't do). All that we do teaches; we are called to be witnesses. We may be the only Bible that some people read.

CATECHISTS: SHARERS OF A WAY OF LIFE

We're involved in far more than instruction. Even people not involved in catechetics have stressed that "education" is more than passing on knowledge.

Important as they are, sharing beliefs, facts, and doctrines is not the totality of our ministry. The *General Directory for Catechesis* (#80) boldly reminds us: "the definite aim of catechesis is to put people not only in touch, but also in communion and intimacy, with Jesus Christ."

A bishop tells the story of when he first went to a new diocese. While visiting various people to get to know the diocese, he went to see the oldest priest.

The bishop asked him, "What has nourished your faith, kept your faith strong, all these years?" The priest, who had served the diocese for seventy years, answered, "My faith is strong because I know someone who knew someone who knew someone who knew someone who knew someone who knew someone who knew Jesus."

Our faith is vibrant because we've known people who knew Jesus. The faith of the people to whom we minister—the adults, the youth, and the children—will be strong because of the people who surround them, people who know Jesus. That's who we are; we are among the people who radiate Jesus to them.

Because of this intimate relationship with Jesus, then, we are impelled to live like Jesus.

Thus, catechesis (what we do) is about sharing the beliefs and tradition, but also, and most emphatically, about empowering practice, a way of living.

CATECHISTS: PROPHETIC VOICES OF HOPE AND COURAGE

Since the Second Vatican Council, the ministry of catechists has often been compared to the role of the biblical prophets. We know that prophets are not fortune tellers, predicting the future. In reality, the prophet helps people to reflect on the experiences of life, seeing them from God's viewpoint, seeking how God is calling them to respond in these events.

In an April 3, 2013, interview with the sister of Pope Francis, Maria Elena Bergoglio speaks about a commitment that might typify the life of a prophet, as she talks about her brother: "his option for the poor. Many times that made his life difficult in Argentina, both in terms of his relationship with the government and also with some businesspeople who wanted him to stop talking about it. But he always chose the poor no matter what, and in this country it can cost you dearly to speak out in favor of the poor."

The role of the catechist calls us always to "look for the more," and to gently challenge those with whom we walk the journey to deeply understand the gospel values, living them in their everyday world.

This quote from Rabbi M. M. Schneerson has always been a challenging reminder to me: "If you see what needs to be repaired and how to repair it, then you have found a piece of the world that God has left for you to complete. But if you only see what is wrong and how ugly it is, then it is yourself that needs repair." As a catechist, how are we always open to seeing what God has called us to heal? As catechists, how do we nudge others to discover their call to rebuild and nurture all things in their everyday world?

In an August 21, 2012, letter to the catechists of his archdiocese of Buenos Aires, then-Cardinal Jorge Mario Bergoglio, now Pope Francis, said: "But catechesis would be seriously compromised if our experience of faith were to leave us confined in and anchored to our familiar world or in the structures and spaces that we have been creating over the years. To believe in the Lord is always to enter anew through the door of faith that makes us go out, to set out on a journey, to leave our comfort zone....We must not forget that the first Christian initiation that occurred in time and in history climaxed in mission...that it took on the characteristics of visitation. With complete clarity the account of Luke tells us: '*Mary arose and went with haste...full of the Spirit.*' "

WHO WE ARE

Perhaps the following anecdote sums up who we are as catechists. (This story tells of the thoughts of a young child; whether we walk this faith journey with children, with youth, or with adults from various perspectives, this could be said about each of us.)

> She was tired. There was work to do at home, at her workplace. She was needed by her family, her parents, her neighbors, her children. There were meetings to attend, sick friends to visit, children to support, encourage, comfort, clean, wash, feed, carpool. She wondered why she had said "Yes."
>
> It was Sunday, Monday, Tuesday, each day and evening of the week. Children, youth, and adults were coming to the parish who wanted to see, who had questions, who needed attention, who wanted to grow. She had done her planning and preparation, but sometimes she wondered if it was worth it.
>
> She was tired. The time for the faith formation sessions had been full, and exhausting. On the way home she hardly heard her son's words as he chattered happily beside her. Then suddenly he caught her attention. "What did you say?" she asked.
>
> "God did not come to class today, so he sent my catechist," her son repeated.
>
> She pulled the car to the curb and hugged her son,

knowing now that walking with others on the faith journey, being a catechist, was worth it all!

Questions for reflection and discussion

- How and when have you felt called to be a catechist?
- What have been, for you, some of the blessings of being a catechist? What have been some of the challenges? As you continue in the future, what will be the blessings? What might some of the challenges be?
- When have you been a companion to someone? Did you bring forth for them something that was already there? Did you receive a gift, something new, from this walk together?
- When and where have you found "a piece of the world that God has left for you to complete"? When and where have you called others to heal a piece of the world?
- What excites you most about your ministry as a catechist?

Things to do

- Describe your "pathway" into becoming—and your journey of being—a catechist. Do it in words, drawing, painting, etc. When and how did you first become aware of your call to be a catechist? How did it develop and grow?

Who was instrumental in helping you to discern that call? Who walked with you? Were there earlier events or experiences in your life that planted the seeds?

- Was there someone who was instrumental in your call to be a catechist? Write them a note thanking them for their support, their encouragement, and their witness.

- Design a symbol that would reflect—for you—who and what a catechist is.

- Gather a few photos or objects that indicate important places and moments in your life. How do these special places and moments affect and relate to your call to be a catechist?

- Is there a quote from this chapter that especially reminds you of who you are as a catechist? Copy it; place it somewhere where you will see it often.

Some characteristics *of a* spirituality *of* catechists

Earlier we reflected on the characteristics of a Catholic Christian spirituality. Those characteristics certainly are also the basis of a spirituality for catechists. Here we consider some additional characteristics. These, of course, are also relevant to all Catholic Christians. Perhaps, in a unique way, though, they can form and strengthen the spirituality of catechists.

As we begin this exploration of the characteristics of a spirituality for catechists, the *National Directory for Catechesis* provides us with a framework:

> "Like all the faithful, catechists are called to holiness. Because of their ministry and mission, however, the call to holiness has a particular urgency. The spiritual life of a catechist should be characterized by:

- A love of God—Father, Son, and Holy Spirit—and of Christ's Church, our Holy Father, and God's holy people

- A coherence and authenticity of life that is characterized by their faithful practice of the faith in a spirit of faith, charity, hope, courage and joy

- Personal prayer and dedication to the evangelizing mission of the Church

- A missionary zeal by which they are fully convinced of the truth of the Catholic faith and enthusiastically proclaim it

- Active participation in their local parish community, especially by attendance at Sunday Eucharist

- A devotion to Mary, the first disciple and the model of catechists, and to the Most Holy Eucharist, the source of nourishment for catechists" (*NDC*, #54B.8)

We have touched upon some of these in our look at the characteristics of a Catholic Christian spirituality. Let's explore a couple of them (here and in our chapter on prayer), as well as a few others that flow from them, which are rooted in who we are called to be as catechists in today's church and world.

EUCHARIST-CENTERED

The spirituality of catechists is centered in Eucharist because of the reality, the mystery, the challenge of what Eucharist is: in receiving the Body of Christ, we become the body of Christ.

When we talk about the "Body of Christ" we are speaking of two mysteries: Jesus' presence in the bread and wine and we who are the body of Christ. It's useless to talk about the "real presence" if we forget that we also are the body of Christ.

The momentous doctrine of the Body of Christ was taught in two different ways by Saint Paul.

He used the term, of course, for the bread and wine of the Eucharist. Paul also used "body of Christ" for the community, building on what Jesus had said, "For where two or three are gathered together in my name, there am I in the midst of them" (Matthew 18:20).

In the early church, when the priest gave Communion saying "Corpus Christi, the Body of Christ," the response was not "Amen" as we now prayerfully respond. The response was "I am"; you, I, we are the body of Christ.

In the first thousand years of our church, the community was called the *Corpus Verum*, the True Body of Christ, and the Eucharist was called the Mystical Body of Christ, *Corpus Mysticum*. Everyone knew that both were the presence of Jesus.

In our second thousand years, the usage almost entirely reversed. The people became the Mystical Body of Christ, and the consecrated bread and wine became *Corpus Verum* or "the real presence."

Centuries ago when Saint Augustine celebrated the Mass and held up the host, he would say: "Receive what you are. Become what you receive." Do we realize today that we are the body of Christ?

During liturgy, the bread and the wine are not the only

things that are changed; we are changed, also, into the body of Christ. Each time we gather to celebrate the Eucharist, our petition during the Eucharistic Prayer asks the Spirit to change the bread and wine into the Body of Christ and to change us into the one body of Christ. The specific words change depending upon which Eucharistic Prayer is used, but the request is always the same: that we who feast on the Body of Christ become the body of Christ!

We often hear the cliché "You are what you eat" and probably imagine that it was coined by a weight-loss clinic. Yet it was first said by Pope Leo the Great when he was talking about receiving Communion. In receiving the Body and Blood of Christ, we choose to become the body of Christ.

If Eucharist makes us the body of Christ, there is an implication, a challenge, for each of us in that. We, as catechists, live that challenge in all we do in our daily lives and in our catechetical ministry.

We act like the body of Christ. We are bread that nourishes others; we are wine that is poured out for others. When we say "Amen," we are not saying it only for the gift of Jesus' presence in Eucharist. It is intentional that the priest or eucharistic minister says "Body of Christ/Blood of Christ" and not "This is the Body of Christ; this is the Blood of Christ."

In this sacred exchange, our "Amen" means that we believe that we are the body of Christ, broken and poured out for others (and that all with us, in this liturgy and in our lives, are the body of Christ).

As catechists, we give our lives for others in nourishment when we

- affirm a woman's insights into how a Scripture passage is alive in her life

- listen to a child's endless questions
- challenge adults, not just to new understandings, but to creative ways of serving
- share Good News with a young person who is searching
- are available to those to whom we minister even "after hours"
- remember (and are concerned about) what is happening in our learners' everyday lives

Our Eucharist-centered spirituality impels us to do, in memory of Jesus, exactly what he did: to be broken and poured out in nourishment, to be a servant to others, to wash the feet of others.

Jesus did two things at the Last Supper: he blessed the bread and wine; he washed the feet of the disciples. The washing of the feet, to be of service to others, is what Eucharist is all about. Eucharist never ends with the act of receiving Communion; we live Eucharist in our 24/7 world.

There's a church in my neighborhood that has one driveway into, and out of, the church property. At the entrance there is a sign saying: "Enter to Worship." As people drive out, a sign reminds them: "Exit to Serve." One of my great-nieces has a T-shirt that says, "What happens in church doesn't stay in church."

In the *Catechism of the Catholic Church* (#1068 and 1136-1140), the church tells us that Eucharist is primarily an action of Christ who gathers the whole community of the baptized to enter into full, conscious, and active participation so that the faithful might go out and be witnesses of Jesus in the world.

Especially for us as catechists, because we have celebrated Eucharist, we are the presence of Jesus in our world. We wash feet; we nourish others in the beliefs we share and with the gospel values we live.

COMMITTED TO GROWTH

All of the characteristics we have looked at (and will continue to peruse) presume a commitment to ongoing growth in our faith journey. And one of the fascinating and rewarding realities for catechists is that the very nature of what we do calls us to ongoing learning. "We learn best what we teach" is a saying that is particularly compelling for our ministry. As we study and prepare for our sessions, whether they be

- a Scripture discussion group for businessmen, or
- a session on God's gift of the seasons for pre-schoolers, or
- an RCIA reflection on the readings of the day, or
- a prayer service on the gifts of the Holy Spirit with our confirmation candidates, or
- an exploration of the many ways we pray for an adult Lenten series,

our own understanding of these themes and new ways of appreciating them continue to grow.

Yet our preparation is only the beginning! The potential for deepened growth also resides in the actual formation gatherings themselves. What a privilege we catechists have to walk with others on the journey of faith. In our role, we are not the experts; we are guides on a mutual journey. Within any and all faith formation opportunities, we all are learners; we learn from each other. "It is in community that catechists test their own vocation and continually nourish their own apostolic awareness" (*General Directory for Catechesis*, #246).

Of course, our continuing growth in faith is much more expansive than these times surrounding our ministry—the planning and leading of our sessions. We are surrounded by a treasury of ways to nourish and nurture our faith: catechist formation programs, online courses, retreats, faith-sharing groups, books and periodicals, days of reflection, workshops, seasonal parish and (arch)diocesan programs, Scripture study, service followed by reflection, etc.

The *General Directory for Catechesis* outlines three dimensions of our ongoing formation as catechists:

- being
- knowing
- savoir-faire (knowing what/how to do something).

> The formation of catechists is made up of different dimensions. The deepest dimension refers to the very *being* of the catechist, to his (her) human and Christian dimension. Formation, above all else, must help him (her) to mature as a person, a believer, and as an apostle. This is what the catechist must *know* so as to be able to fulfill his (her) responsibilities well. This dimension is permeated by the double commitment he (she) has to the message and to man (humanity). It requires the catechist to have a sufficient knowledge of the message that he (she) transmits and of those to whom he (she) transmits the message and of the social context in which they live. This then is the dimension of savoire-faire, of *knowing how to* transmit the message, so that it is an act of communication. (#238)

Realizing who we are, understanding the message, and developing our skills to teach, to facilitate, and to walk with others—these are our three vital areas of growth. This is certainly a challenge, but also a gift of deepening, a gift of appreciating and participating in experiences of expanding our faith and our privilege of sharing it.

HOSPITALITY

In an August 21, 2012, letter to the catechists of Buenos Aires, then-Cardinal Jorge Mario Bergoglio, now Pope Francis, said: "Thank you for your quiet, faithful work each week, for your ability to be Good Samaritans who offer hospitality out of faith, by being familiar faces and dear hearts..." The church—each parish and (arch)diocese—is called to be welcoming and hospitable. Catechists have a unique opportunity (and challenge) to be this symbol and reality of welcome and hospitality to so many today.

In both the Old Testament and the New Testament, it is easy to see that hospitality expresses people's relationship with God and one another. The Acts of the Apostles is a story of how Christianity was spread because of the hospitality of local Christian communities.

In our world today, often when we hear the word "hospitality," our thoughts immediately go to refreshments, to food and drink. That is an extremely important part of hospitality, but the spirit of welcome reaches far beyond.

- Hospitality is evident in our smile, in our attitude of joy, in our delight in the gifts and presence of each and every person.

- Hospitality is evident in our desire and commitment to listen. As Saint John Paul II wrote in *Novo Millennio Ineunte*, quoting Saint Paulinus of Nola: "Let us listen to what all the faithful say, because in every one of them the Spirit of God breathes" (no. 45).

- Hospitality is evident in the continual and constant ways we convey to people that they are worthwhile. Our actions, as well as our words, authentically communicate this.

- Hospitality is evident in our remembering: remembering what is happening in people's lives, taking time to inquire about people's joys and struggles, and connecting real life with faith in all we do.

- Hospitality is evident in our encouraging words, our supportive actions, and our compassionate spirit.

KINDNESS

Henry James, the American novelist, said: "Three things in human life are important. The first is to be kind. The second is to be kind. And the third is to be kind."

Sometimes we might think of kindness as just a simple word, even a practice that's childish, something we tell children to do, or one of the blander virtues, lacking charisma or clout. Near the end of his life, Rabbi Abraham Heschel said: "When I was young, I used to admire intelligent people; as I grow older, I admire kind people."

Scripture reminds us: "Put on then, as God's chosen ones, holy and beloved, heartfelt compassion, kindness, humility, gentleness, and patience" (Colossians 3:12).

All, of course, are called to kindness. For catechists, kindness is embedded in our spirituality. We have responded to the call in kindness, the desire to give what we have been given.

We live kindness in all we do—in the ways we relate to others. Centuries ago, Plato said: "Be kind, for everyone you meet is fighting a hard battle." We might not always know the struggles, the discouragements, the disappointments, and the losses of those to whom we minister in catechetics. Yet our life and manner of kindness touches their day and models for them the kindness and care of our ever-present God.

Joan Chittister, in *A High Spiritual Season,* reminds us of the challenge to be kind: "We must be very careful, for prayer can be an easy substitute for real spirituality. It would be impossible to have spirituality without prayer, of course, but it is certainly possible to pray without having a spirituality at all. How do you know? 'Am I becoming kinder?' is a good place to start."

JOY

One of my favorite books to read with my great-nieces and great-nephews is *Alexander and the Terrible, Horrible, No Good, Very Bad Day*. When my great-nephew Tyler was three and four years old, he wouldn't let me read it to him. He would emphatically respond, "It's not a bad day; it's a very good day. Look at all the great things we have and can do." What joy!

When someone asked Saint John XXIII why he called the Second Vatican Council, he immediately responded: "to make the human sojourn a little less sad." Pope John realized that for most (all) people, their lives contain worries and the strains of everyday life. It is one of the roles of the church to accompany people on this journey, enabling the journey to be a little lighter, a little more joyful.

G. K. Chesterton reminds us: "As Christians, joy is the underlying pulsation of our life." This does not mean that we don't experience pain, suffering, and anxieties. In the midst of these, the Christian story, especially the Easter story, shouts to us that our tears and anguishes can be transformative, redemptive. New life is always present! God shows, in raising Jesus from the dead, that new life overpowers death, and joy overcomes sorrow.

The word "joy" appears in Scripture more than 315 times. What a gift we have; what a challenge we have been given.

Pope Francis (in his 2012 letter to catechists when he was Cardinal Jorge Mario Bergoglio) said to us:

> It is good to realize that today, more than ever, the act of believing must allow the joy of the Faith to shine through. As in that joyous encounter of Mary and Elizabeth, the catechist must imbue his or her entire person and ministry with the joy of the Faith. Allow me to share something of what we bishops of Argentina wrote a few months ago in a document in which we sketch some common pastoral guidelines for the three-year period 2012-2015:
>
> > *Joy is the door for the proclamation of the Good News and also for the consequence of living in faith. It is the expression that opens the way to receive the love of God who is Father of all. Thus we note in the Annunciation of the angel to the Virgin Mary that, before telling her what was going to happen to her, he invites her to be filled with joy. And this is also Jesus' message when he invites people to trust and to an encounter with God the Father: rejoice. This Christian joy is a gift of God that springs naturally from the personal encounter with the Risen Christ and faith in him.*
>
> Therefore I gladly exhort you with the Apostle Paul: "Rejoice, rejoice always in the Lord...." May the catechesis that you serve so lovingly be marked by this joy, the fruit of the nearness of the

> Risen Lord ("the disciples were glad when they saw the Lord," Jn 20:20), which also allows others to discover your goodness and your readiness to respond to the Lord's call....

The ancient Egyptians believed that, when they died, they would be asked two questions. Their answers would determine whether they continued their journey in the afterlife. These two questions were: "Did you find joy?" and "Did you bring joy?" These are wonderful questions for catechists, aren't they?

Blessed Julian of Norwich said, "The greatest honor you can give to Almighty God is to live gladly, joyfully, because of the knowledge of God's love." Our joy is anchored in that experience of love; as catechists it exudes from us, touching so many others. That is our call. Saint Francis of Assisi said, "Our job is to lift up people's hearts and give them reasons for spiritual joy." As adults, youth, or children leave our catechetical sessions, do they leave with spiritual joy?

GRATITUDE

There's a Jewish folktale which tells about a young man who aspired to great holiness. After some time working to achieve it, he went to see his rabbi. "Rabbi," he announced, "I think I have achieved sanctity."

"Why do you think that?" asked the Rabbi.

"Well," replied the young man, "I've been practicing virtue and discipline for some time and I have grown quite proficient at them. From the time the sun rises until it sets, I take no food or water. All day long, I do all kinds of hard work for others and I never expect to be thanked. When I have temptations, I roll in the snow or the thorn bushes until they go away, and then at night, before bed, I practice an ancient monastic discipline and administer lashes to my bare back. I have disciplined myself so as to be holy."

The rabbi was silent for a time. Then he took the young man by the arm and led him to the window, pointing to an old horse which was just being led away by its master.

"I have been observing that horse for some time," the rabbi said, "and I have noticed that it doesn't get fed or watered from morning to night. All day long it has to do work for people and it never gets thanked. I often see it rolling around in the snow or bushes, as horses are prone to do, and frequently I see it get whipped. But, I ask you: is that a saint or a horse?"

To be a saint is to be motivated by gratitude. Gratitude is the basic Christian attitude, a foundational characteristic of our spirituality. Meister Eckhart profoundly says, "If the only prayer you ever say is 'thank you,' that is enough."

There is more and more being written today—books, articles, blogs—which tell about the research being done proving that grateful people are healthier physically, emotionally, intellectually, and spiritually. How important it is for us, since it is embedded in who we are as Catholic Christians. Paul tells the Thessalonians: "In all circumstances give thanks, for this is the will of God for you in Christ Jesus" (1 Thessalonians 5:18).

Our very being, our deepest way of prayer, is about gratitude. Each week we celebrate Eucharist; *eucharist* is a Greek word that means "thanksgiving." We may think of many, many reasons why we worship each weekend (or daily). They would all be true, yet the main reason is we gather to give thanks. Despite our disappointments, discouragements, losses, and worries, we have, at the same time, been given so much. All that we can do in the face of such a gracious gift is to say thank you to our God.

The Zen master Ryokan came home one night to discover that robbers had stolen everything from his simple hut.

Standing in the midst of his small home, with everything gone, he exclaimed, "They left the best thing—the moon at the window!" Make a list of your "best things." How do you express gratitude for them?

To be a catechist rooted in our spirituality is to be motivated by gratitude. Gratefulness connects us to God, the generous giver of all good things. Gratitude empowers us to see each person with whom we walk the journey of faith as a gift. Thanksgiving instills in us an attitude of respect, joy, and wonder at all that happens, especially within our ministry as catechists.

SITUATIONAL SPIRITUALITY

Perhaps catechists have a situational spirituality.

In many ways, this is an integration of many of the characteristics we have already talked about (and will continue to look at when we reflect on prayer and spiritual practices): seeing the sacred in the ordinary, seeing with God's eyes, responding compassionately, being companions on the journey, staying committed to growth, living life gratefully, etc.

Situational spirituality is an integrated life, a cohesive spirituality. We find the depths of our spirituality within the real life situations that already make up our lives. Everyone can live this type of spirituality:

- Becoming aware of stress prompts a few minutes of prayerful meditation
- Driving in the car provides a chance for reflection on the day's activities
- Running into an old friend unexpectedly brings forth a prayer of gratitude
- Failing to respond to someone's needs leads to a longing for forgiveness

- Feeling anxious or worried produces a petition for peace and strength
- Boredom with television leads to a half hour of spiritual reading
- Insightful conversations with friends flow into prayerful journal writing

Perhaps catechists are surrounded by the privilege of situational spirituality, not only in their everyday lives, but uniquely in their lives and ministry as a catechist. Have you ever experienced:

- Planning a prayer service for engaged couples in the premarriage program, which became prayer for you?
- Listening to a catechumen speak of their journey of faith, which led you to a grateful remembering of your own journey?
- Studying Scripture in preparation for a Scripture study for mothers of young children, which opened new insights into God's word for you?
- Watching the enthusiasm of young children paint their feelings about God's love, which unearthed ardent feelings in you?
- Answering the questions of youth about suffering and loss, which prompted a quick prayer for help and wisdom?
- Facilitating an absorbing discussion during an Advent retreat, which led you to prayers of gratitude?
- Studying the needs of today and Catholic social teaching as you prepared for a session, which impelled you to reach out in service and justice?

Spirituality is all-inclusive; it flows from and touches all parts of life. To be committed, faith-filled disciples, we need to be intentional about taking time to nurture our spirituality. At the same time, our spirituality—who we are—is nurtured and grows continually and constantly. As catechists, we experience the privilege of growth because of, and within, our ministry.

Questions for reflection and discussion

- Which of the characteristics in the *National Catechetical Directory* best describe you? Why? Which of the characteristics provide the biggest challenge for you? How might you work on them this year?
- How do you model and exude hospitality within your catechetical sessions?
- Recall your childhood. Remember especially a parish catechist or Catholic schoolteacher who overflowed with joy. What was the source of her or his joy?
- When was the last time you thanked God? When was the last time you thanked someone in your life, someone close to you or someone in passing who simply did a kind act for you?
- What, in your daily life, calls you to prayer, to awareness of God, to connection with others, to a deepening spirituality? What, in your ministry as a catechist, calls you to prayer, to awareness of God, to connection with others, to a deepening spirituality?

Things to do

- With another catechist, choose something you will do together that will deepen your spirituality.
- Invite a friend to lunch. During your conversation ask that person what she or he is reading. Share a book that has deepened your spiritual life.
- Is there one person in your catechetical sessions who especially needs welcoming and hospitality right now?
- At the end of each day ask yourself: what three things brought me genuine joy today? Decide upon one thing you could do (anonymously) to bring joy to someone else.
- Begin a journal of things for which you are grateful. Each night before you go to bed, write down three things from that day. One way to give thanks to God is to thank the people in our lives. Decide to write one thank you note each month (or each week).

Prayer *as a* foundational practice

It has been said that if you asked twelve people for their definition of prayer, you'd probably end up with thirteen definitions. Prayer is a mystery; it is something that can't be captured in words. In reality, when we are speaking about prayer, we are talking about three mysteries.

First, prayer is concerned with ourselves, who we are. We are always learning something new about what it means to be human. Second, prayer is certainly about God. Will we ever know and understand everything about God? What an awesome mystery we connect with when we are united to God. Third, prayer is about a relationship. As you think about the person closest to you, is your relationship the same today as it was ten years ago, four years ago, last year, even three weeks ago? Relationships are always evolving and changing.

Thus, when we talk about prayer, we're talking about a mystery that encompasses these three unique mysteries (and perhaps even more).

Therefore, trying to place prayer into one definition can be very limiting. The *United States Catholic Catechism for Adults* affirms this when it says: "Descriptions of prayer are abundant throughout Christian history....Definitions of prayer are important, but insufficient" (page 463).

When we define prayer, it seems as though we take one (very true) idea about prayer, but imply that this says everything about prayer. If we defined "sports" by saying "sports is baseball," we would be leaving out swimming, skating, handball, and a number of other realities of today's sports. When we say "prayer is talking to God," that is certainly true. At the same time, does it leave out other realities of the mystery of prayer?

A DESCRIPTION OF PRAYER

Even though spirituality encompasses all of life, it is obvious that prayer is foundational to spirituality. If we choose not to define prayer, what helps us to think about, understand, and appreciate the mystery and gift of prayer? The key is to always remember that there are many ways to describe prayer. This mystery calls forth many images and depictions. The gift is that each description allows us to understand the mystery of prayer through another lens, another facet.

One way of describing prayer is that prayer is everything and anything that helps us to recognize what we already have. We are already in the presence of God; we are always one with God; we are continually united with God. Prayer helps to bring to our awareness this cherished connection that we have with God.

Thomas Merton said: "In prayer we discover what we already have. We already have everything, but we don't know it and we don't experience what we already possess. The whole thing boils down to giving ourselves in prayer a chance to realize that we have what we seek. We don't have to rush after it. It is there all the time, and if we give it time it will make itself known to us."

If there's a challenge in this description of prayer, perhaps it is with us. We are not aware enough. Do we always realize how close our God is to us?

One description of prayer, therefore, is that prayer is about awareness. Prayer helps us to become more aware of life, of who we are, of whose we are. In all parts of our lives, we need to be more aware. As disciples of Jesus, we especially are called to be aware of the closeness of our God, to recognize, to feel, and to hear God within our lives, within our world.

A parable tells of two little fish who met a frog beneath a rock. The frog exclaimed: "Don't you know you're in great danger, little fishes?"

Extremely frightened, the fish cried, "No!"

"Don't you know fish can't live without water?" teased the cruel frog. "You'd better find some water quickly or you'll die."

The little fish quickly swam home to their mother in great distress. "Oh Mother, Mother," they cried. "The frog says if we don't find some water quickly, we'll die. Mother, what's water?"

"I don't know," confessed the mother fish (who was an agnostic). "I've never heard anything about water. Let's go and ask the otter."

As they arrived at the otter's home and asked their question, the otter laughed. "Water, my dears? Why, you live in water! That's what you breathe!"

We live in God. That's what we breathe.

Prayer helps us to recognize what we already have. Prayer is a tool we have for walking in God's presence. Ultimately, we pray so that we don't lose consciousness of God's always-near presence.

In reality, prayer is not to get something. Prayer is, simply and deeply, to remind us who we are, whose we are. Prayer is, according to our culture's usual standards, a waste of time. Prayer is not for something. Prayer is not about finding God or coming into God's presence, for we're already there. Prayer is about recognizing the divine presence that is so close to us.

God-with-us is so interrelated in our daily lives that, perhaps, we have learned to take it for granted. If you held this book up right now very close to your face, practically touching your nose, you couldn't read it. It's too close. Does that happen at times with our awareness of God? Do we fail to see God because God is always so intimately near to us?

We are not called to "do prayers," but to be prayerful people. When we describe prayer in this way we realize that there are many possibilities for prayer, many ways to pray. Saint Ignatius of Loyola reminded us: "Everything that turns a person in the direction of God is prayer."

Prayer, in its many forms, helps us to appreciate the dazzling simplicity of ordinary life. Prayer helps us to experience, ever more deeply, the wonder of life: we are always and everywhere in the presence of God.

In the book *Healing Words: The Power of Prayer and the Practice of Medicine*, Dr. Larry Dossey visits a man dying of a terminal illness and asks him, "What do you pray for?"

The man replied: "I don't pray for anything. How would I know what to ask for?"

Dr. Dossey was surprised; surely this dying man had some requests on his mind. Dr. Dossey inquired, "If prayer is not for asking, what is it for?"

The man quietly answered, "It isn't for anything. It mainly reminds me I am not alone."

Prayer, then, is a means to the end, not the end itself. The reason for prayer, the end we search for, the reason we pray, is to more and more deeply become aware of, to come into friendship and unity with, our compassionate God, who is always present.

THE CHALLENGE OF PRAYER

Prayer reminds me of whose I am; prayer reminds me of my close, never-ending union with God. Does that make a difference in my life? Does it call me to be someone, to do something?

Centuries ago, Saint Augustine said: "Pray as though everything depended upon God. Work as though everything depended upon you." Once upon a time there was a farm that had been for sale for a long time. In the absence of owners, the fields were not tended, becoming overrun with weeds and debris. The farm was finally purchased by an energetic young man who worked tirelessly on the buildings and the acres of fields. One day he was in town at the general store purchasing more supplies when a neighboring farmer approached him. The farmer welcomed him to the area and said, "Wow, that place was a mess. You and God did a good job with those fields." The young man smiled and replied, "You should have seen it when God had it all by himself."

Prayer presupposes a commitment on our part to assume responsibility for what we are praying for, a commitment to be part of the solution.

In reality, we cannot pray for someone; we do not pray for a need; we only pray with. We cannot avoid the company of those who suffer, those who are in need. Prayer calls us to action. If we pray for someone who is sick, but never send a card, never call or visit, never help his or her family, are we really praying? Are our words (in prayer) calling us to do something (to live our prayer)? C.S. Lewis remarked once: "I am often, I believe, praying for others when I should be doing things for them. It's so much easier to pray for a bore than to go and see him."

Our prayers of petition—important as they are—should not be giving God good advice on how to run the world, such as,

"God, help those in the third world find enough to eat"; "God, please put an end to violence."

Friends of mine who pray a prayer similar to the liturgy's General Intercessions at their evening meal were stopped one night by their nine-year-old as he said, "I think we're praying all wrong." The other family members weren't sure what to say; Timmy's mother finally asked, "How do you think we should be praying, Timmy?"

Timmy replied, "We're praying for the poor people so that they have enough food. We're praying for Mrs. Downey next door so she won't be lonely because her husband died. I think we should pray that we have the generosity to buy some good food, take it to the soup kitchen, and help serve the meals. I think we should pray that we make the time to invite Mrs. Downey for dinner with us once a week."

Each passage in the New Testament about the prayer of petition is connected with a statement about fraternal charity. We are the hands and ears of God. And if we don't listen, God can't hear. If we don't act, God can't bring reconciliation, help, and strength. The Christ who answers prayers is we who act as the Body of Christ.

God cannot do for us what God cannot do through us. It's like a building that is wired for electricity, but still needs lighting fixtures and lamps if the building is to be lit. We are the hands and ears of God. We can't just pray and then forget about the people and the needs for which we prayed. There is a wise proverb that challenges us: "Prayer without action is like drawing water with a woven basket."

Immediately after a phone call about a friend who is suffering, pray and decide how you will contact her or him. Amid the news headlines that speak of war, pray to be a peacemaker. Hearing about conditions of the poor in your city, pray to be an advocate for them. Frustrated by political leaders, pray to be an active citizen, working for change.

Saint John Chrysostom prompted us: "The sincerity of our prayer is determined by our willingness to work on its behalf." Saint Thomas More prayed, "The things, good Lord, that I pray for, give me your grace to labor for."

WAYS OF PRAYER

The *United States Catholic Catechism for Adults* tells us that "there is a huge difference between knowing about prayer and praying. On this issue, the Rule of Saint Benedict is clear: 'If a man (woman) wants to pray, let him (her) go and pray'" (page 463). We could fill whole bookstores with the amount of books (and articles, internet sites, and blogs) that have been and are being written about prayer, especially about the various forms and methods of prayer.

Many years ago, I participated in a week-long retreat/workshop that centered on the Myers-Briggs Type Indicator and its relationship to spirituality and prayer. A friend of mine, a sister in my community, was also attending.

About half-way through the week, Jean said to me, "Janet, this is the most freeing thing I've ever experienced. I am so grateful."

When I asked her what she meant, she replied, "For the first forty years of my religious life, I thought I was a bad nun. Now, here this week, I realize that in those days (prior to the Second Vatican Council) when we all prayed exactly the same way, and it never varied, we were praying in a way that was far from the preference of my personality type. I didn't have an opportunity to pray in those years with the forms and types of prayer that connected and resonated with my personality. After the Council, as we, like many others, began to rediscover the rich heritage of prayer within our tradition and retained our prayer forms of the past, but also added to them, I discovered all the vast and precious forms of prayer we have."

The conversation with Jean and especially her experience of not feeling worthy left an indelible memory with me. What an astounding, humbling responsibility and challenge we have.

Prayer is certainly and foremost our union with God and our openness to God who loves us beyond words, more than we can even begin to wrap our minds around.

At the same time, prayer is also and always formative. Every time we pray, we are formed; something happens to us. We are changed; our perceptions change; who we are changes. Our prayer changes (and grows); our relationship with God changes.

As Catholic Christians today, we are immersed in a rich, exquisite tradition of prayer. What a privilege it is to experience the many methods of prayer (as well as to pass them on to all with whom we journey). What a responsibility to learn about and pray the many forms, finding the ones that especially help us to deepen our relationship with God and all in God's family. As catechists (whether with adults, youth, children, families, etc.), can we share with our people, pray with them, many of the various ways and methods of prayer in our tradition? If we pray with them the same way each time we meet, what will happen for those people for whom that type of prayer doesn't connect with their personality? Sharing with them, praying with them, in a diversity of formats provides experiences of the rich treasure of our prayer tradition.

A few of the many ways of prayer: Listed here are some of the many ways of prayer. Which are important to you? Which new ones might you try?

Blessings
Centering Prayer
Charismatic Prayer
Contemplative Prayer
Devotions
Eucharistic Adoration
Evening Prayer
Examen of Consciousness
Examination of Conscience
Faith-Sharing Prayer
Fallow Time: The Prayer of Doing Nothing
The Jesus Prayer
Journaling
Labyrinth Prayer
Lectio Divina
Listening Prayer
Litanies
The Liturgy
Liturgy of the Hours
Mantras
Meal Prayer and Rituals
Meditation
Morning Prayer
Music and Song
Novenas
Photography as Prayer
The Prayer of Everyday Experiences
Prayer Groups
Prayer of Silence
Prayer with Gestures
Prayer Walking
Praying in/with Nature
Praying through Written Words
Prayer while Reading the Newspaper
Praying with Art (other's)
Praying with Art (one's own)
Praying with Dreams
Praying with Gestures and Movement
Praying with Images/Icons
Praying with/because of Interruptions
Praying with Mandalas
Praying with Memories
Praying with Scripture
Praying with the Psalms
Praying with the Saints
The Rosary
Sacraments
Scriptural Meditation
The Spiritual Exercises of Saint Ignatius
Spontaneous Prayer
Stations of the Cross
Taizé Prayer
Traditional (memorized) Prayer
Using Technology to Pray
Visio Divina

SOME SPECIFIC WAYS OF PRAYER FOR CATECHISTS

Many of the ways of prayer can be adapted specifically for our lives as catechists.

Praying within the Communion of Saints: Sr. Jose Hobday, OSF, an author and international speaker on prayer and spirituality, spoke of a prayer method she used while praying alone (yet also praying within the community of saints). Jose imagined herself as part of a large circle. Within the circle she visualized many people: wisdom figures within the community (past and present), people who were important to her, people who had connections with her. She prayed in the presence, and with the support, of all these people.

As catechists, who might be within our prayer circle—patron saints of catechists (Saint Robert Bellarmine and Saint Charles Borromeo), the patron saints of our learners, the families, especially the ancestors, of our learners, those who have mentored us?

Journaling: We live in such a hurried world that we need to intentionally make the time for reflection on our lives. For many people, journal-writing is a method that slows them down for this type of contemplation. As catechists, we might journal about our experiences:

- Giving thanks for people, happenings, and encounters
- Naming the challenges ahead, praying for God's strength and wisdom
- Bringing to mind people on the journey with us who have asked for prayer
- Remembering the concerns, worries, and dreams of those with whom and to whom we minister

One of my journals simply lists those people and circumstances that I am currently keeping in prayer. Praying with this on my lap, and perusing it often, also reminds me to reach out to them in ways of concern and care.

Scripture: No matter what age group we are ministering to and with as a catechist, Scripture is a part of our prayer, our reflection, our learning. Each week, as you begin to plan your catechetical gathering, look ahead for the Scripture reading(s) that will be used. Use these in your prayer—not studying them (at this time) but praying with them. Ask yourself: what is God's message to me in this passage?

Composing a Creed: Write a creed praying about your beliefs concerning the catechetical ministry of the church and your role in it. As you pray it periodically, your new experiences might suggest new certainties and values that you would want to add to it.

Intercessory Prayer: Make a list of those people (adults, youth, and/or children) in your care as catechist. Place it where you will see it every day (or many times a day). Praying for those with whom we journey can affect the way we minister.

In addition to praying for each of them as a group, at times pray for one person at a time. Keep each person individually in your prayer and thoughts for a specific week (or a day). As part of your prayer, you might want to send the person a written note, letting them know that you prayed for them during the week and thanking them for the gifts that they bring to your learning group.

I have a friend who remembers the people for whom she is praying by tying a small piece of colored yarn to her steering wheel—a different color for each person. Are there people with you on this journey of faith (co-catechists, mentors, learners, etc.) for whom you are especially praying? Would doing this—or something similar—be a prayer reminder for you?

Praying While Catechizing: Everything can call us to prayer. In the midst of a session, when you are in awe of the enthusiastic faith of your learners, whisper a prayer of thanks. When something occurs, a question is asked, and you're not sure what to do next, ask for God's words and wisdom.

PRAYER: WHEN AND HOW?

As we conclude this reflection on prayer, I am reminded of a friend of mine, a devoted catechist working with adults, who pondered some of her experiences of prayer:

> I am a "returned" Catholic, having left in my 20s and 30s. My "day job" is as a pilot. I have spent the last thirty-two years with a major carrier flying all over the country. One of my most special "prayer places" is 35,000 feet, in the quiet and calm when God is palpably present. (This is never a distraction, nor does it cause inattentiveness during busy times! I don't reveal this place often for that reason.) I have been immersed in those pink clouds others see from the ground, seen lightning fill huge billowing clouds, and had a front seat to some of the most awe-inspiring views of creation.
>
> I am considering retiring at this point, and part of my reticence is that I will miss this "prayer place." I have discussed this with a mentor who asked: "What exactly is it about that place and your connection in prayer? When you are outdoors hiking, for instance, why don't you feel the same connection?" The question has taken me awhile to work through, but what I have come to realize is that during those years when I was away from my faith, that was the one place where I never lost my connection to God. If God never

crossed my mind during all my other activities, I never forgot when I witnessed the world from above. That was where God "held" on to me. God holds on to me in so many ways now that I realize I can leave that place with a sense of peace.

Now I realize that I have reestablished a prayer life that includes more places and faces. Growing up I thought of prayer as something done in church or on your knees at night. Now I know that prayer is found everywhere, in some interesting places, and it certainly isn't all just words.

Some of my favorite prayers are quite diverse:

- Feeding and watering the horses each evening: a prayer for the beauty of the creatures with which we share this space.
- Doing the laundry and ironing: how we care for one another, over and over again.
- Drawing, painting, practicing the piano: have you ever felt "part" of the music, even just for a fraction of a second?
- Walking in an urban area: looking into every face that passes and saying silently, "There is the face of God." I can only do this for short periods because it is quite emotionally overwhelming at times, especially when I pass the homeless.
- Praying with Scripture: I find myself going back to some readings over and over.
- Praying community prayers in echoes or in different languages at the same time: I love to feel "surrounded" by the many voices and tones, wrapped in prayer.

Questions for reflection and discussion

- What are your favorite ways of praying?
- Do you have —or have you had—a prayer place where you felt God palpably present?
- Who first taught you to pray?
- Whom do you pray to?
- How has prayer changed you?

Things to do

- Who is a prayerful person that you know? What do you notice about him or her? Be gently observant in the next few weeks of people in your life. Do you notice prayerful people? How do you recognize them?
- Learn about a prayer method that you have never used before; try that prayer way and see if it resonates with you.
- Set up some "triggers" for prayer. For example: a prayer or Scripture verse taped to a mirror, your steering wheel, the refrigerator.
- Decide on a specific way you will pray for those to whom you minister in your catechetical session(s).

Some other practices *to* deepen *and* live our spirituality

There is an old story of a young violinist who had an audition at Carnegie Hall. As she hurriedly exited the subway, she was momentarily disoriented. Seeing an elderly gentleman with a violin under his arm, she asked, "Sir, can you tell me how to get to Carnegie Hall?"

With a caring smile, he replied, "Practice."

Throughout our history, we have realized that certain practices help connect us deeply to who we are, whose we are, and who we're called to be. A spiritual practice is a regular pattern in our lives that brings us back to the present moment. It is a habit that brings us back to God. It is a tool for becoming more and more aware of God within the everyday moments of our lives.

As Richard Rohr and Saint Thomas Aquinas said above, we don't think about our beliefs or practices for a few moments each day and then return to "the rest of our lives." Practice is what we're all about. How do all the practices of our day—and life—affect how we behave with our family during a rushed morning, respond in a traffic jam, react to a homeless person asking for help, care for the hurting, listen when we're tired, etc.?

Our spirituality is just that: our living of a spirit-filled life. Our living of our spirituality, through all the practices of our life, enables us to arrive at a faith that is deeper than our learning. What we believe is our religion; who we are, what we live for, how we live, is faith, a faith and deep spirituality that see us through, that challenge us to live as disciples.

SOME OF OUR SPIRITUALITY PRACTICES

Listed here (in addition to the various prayer ideas in the previous chapter) are a few—of the many—spiritual practices that Christians find helpful, as they continually root themselves in their spirituality of connectedness to God and others, and live that compassionate care in their everyday world.

Awareness of God's presence throughout the day
Awareness of myself as sacrament
Book clubs
Care of creation
Care of the gift of my body
Celebrating of life, special events
Continual learning/formation
Creating sacred space
Discernment
Fasting
Forgiveness
Gardening
Giving generously
Justice work
Listening to a friend
Listening to music
Liturgical Year rituals & celebrations
Living gratefully
Living in the present moment
Living sacramentally (seeing the holy all around)
Living simply
Making friends with people who are different
Mantra for the day/the week
Mindfulness
Participating in community
Pilgrimages
Placing no borders on my concern and prayers
Play
Practicing hospitality
Random acts of kindness
Reading
Retreats

Reverence
Sabbath moments
Savoring beauty
Seeing work as part of my spirituality
Seasonal celebrations and rituals
Self-care
Service
Silence
Spiritual direction
Spiritual mentors and companions
Spiritual reading
Story-telling
Suffering
Suffering with and for one another
Times of silence
Use of sacramentals
Volunteering

SOME SPIRITUAL PRACTICES PERSONALIZED FOR CATECHISTS

Many spiritual practices can be adapted specifically for our lives as catechists. They can open us to a deepening of our call and ministry.

Mantra for the day/the week: What's the "sound track," the message that we have—often unconsciously—playing in our minds? Is it one of worry, of negativity, of fear? Rather, do we have a comforting and enthusiastic phrase we can repeat to ourselves as we go throughout the day, especially in the times of our ministry?

We can use short phrases based on Scripture passages:

- I will not leave you orphaned.
- You are my beloved son/daughter.
- I am with you until the end.
- You are worth more than many sparrows.
- I have called you by name; you are mine.
- As you have received a gift, use it to serve.
- I will teach you in the way you should go.
- Be steadfast in the work of the Lord.
- For nothing will be impossible with God.
- I have not stopped giving thanks for you.
- The one who calls me is faithful.

What about the psalm response from each Sunday liturgy? These powerful—comforting and challenging—prayers can become our refrain in the background of our days during the week, during our ministry.

Faith-sharing: All that we do in our ministry as catechists is share faith. Do we also, in our everyday lives, find people with whom we can share our story? When we share faith with another we speak and hear the "word of God" as it has entered each of our lives. Each of us has our own "salvation history" that tells of the ways in which God has been real in our lives and in our catechetical ministry. This history, our experiences and their meaning, deepens when we share it, when we listen to the experiences of others.

Moments of silence: We live in a busy, noisy world. Moments of silence can reveal to us the wonders of our God, the miracles of everyday life, and the surprises and gifts within our ministry as catechists.

Are we also too talkative in prayer? A five-year-old asked me once, "Why is prayer so noisy?" Listening to God in prayer—rather than doing all the talking—opens all kinds of marvelous astonishments.

Living in the present moment: God cannot find us where we think we ought to be. God can only find us where we are. The Sufi mystic says, "The place where you are right now, God circled on a map for you."

How often do we live in the past ("if only that hadn't happened") or the future (planning what we'll do in three hours, or tomorrow, or next year)? God was in the past and will be in the future, but the only place where God is now is in the present.

A growing spirituality calls us to live in and appreciate the now, just as Emily in *Our Town* realized after her death. As she returned to earth, revisiting her twelfth birthday, she realized that "Grover's Corners...Mama and Papa...clocks ticking and Mama's sunflowers...food and coffee...new-ironed dresses and hot baths...and sleeping and waking up" are gifts "too wonderful for anybody to realize."

Emily asked, "Do any human beings ever realize life while they live it—every, every minute?" The stage manager responds, "No. The saints and poets, maybe—they do some."

Our call to live and cherish the present moment surrounds us 24/7/365. Simple things and extraordinary things touch us as we live in the now: a tender touch, the beauty of a face, a child's unconditional love, the gift of forgiveness, an offer to help, God's Word alive in each happening. In our ministry—when we're preparing sessions, when we're in our catechetical gatherings—are we living in the moment? Are we aware of the gifts, of the touch of God, in each moment? Are we attentive to the people, their needs, feelings, questions, and experiences; are we intent on the sights, sounds, and sensations of the lives all around us? Grace seizes us in the present moment.

Questions for reflection and discussion

- What spiritual practices have been or are now especially important for you?

- How do you—in our busy world—meet the challenge of finding time for prayer, for reflection, for spiritual practices? What are the particular challenges for you? What are the blessings and gifts? What are your secrets for finding time?

- What happens to you when you listen in prayer rather than doing all the talking?

- What do you do each day (or each week) to live gratefully? How does this impact your catechetical ministry?

- What helps have you found to anchor yourself in the present moment, throughout all life and in the moments of your catechetical ministry?

Things to do

- Choose a spiritual practice that has never been a part of your life, but which interests you. See what happens when you take time to incorporate it into your life.

- Choose a mantra—perhaps a line from Scripture—to run in the background of your day, to support you in your catechetical ministry.

- Ask a family member, a friend, another catechist, etc., about their favorite spiritual practices. What helps them to stay rooted in God?

- Justice work, service, and giving generously are spiritual practices that are integral to our baptismal promises and to our witness as catechists. Decide on one new way you might reach out in the weeks ahead.